Days
of
Memory

Days of Memory

Listening to Jewish Italians who lived through Fascism and the Holocaust

Judith Monachina

White River Press
Amherst, Massachusetts

First published 2024 by White River Press
Amherst, Massachusetts • whiteriverpress.com

ISBN: 979-8-88545-005-8

Book and cover design by Lufkin Graphic Designs
Norwich, Vermont • www.LufkinGraphics.com

Permissions:

Photos: Virginia Gattegno Cipolato, USC Shoah Foundation Visual History Archive

Guido Weiller, Contemporary Jewish Documentation Center (CDEC), Milan

Liliana Picciotto, by Sara Fargion.

Library of Congress Cataloging-in-Publication Data

Names: Monachina, Judith, 1960- author.
Title: Days of memory : listening to Jewish Italians who lived through
   fascism and the Holocaust / Judith Monachina.
Other titles: Listening to Jewish Italians who lived through fascism and
   the Holocaust
Description: Amherst, Massachusetts : White River Press, 2024. | Includes
   bibliographical references and index.
Identifiers: LCCN 2024003733 | ISBN 9798885450058 (paperback)
Subjects: LCSH: Jews--Italy--Interviews. | Holocaust
   survivors--Italy--Interviews. | Holocaust, Jewish
   (1939-1945)--Italy--Personal narratives. |
   Jews--Persecutions--Italy--History--20th century. | Jews
   Italy--History--20th century. | Italy--Ethnic relations.
Classification: LCC DS135.I8 M626 2024 | DDC 909/.04924--dc23/
eng/20240205
LC record available at https://lccn.loc.gov/2024003733

Contents

Part Two: In the Place of Memory

Part Three: A Postlude

Prologue

September 8, 1943, is etched clearly in the minds of those who lived through it in Italy. Mention this date to anyone and they will remember the chaos, the minutes—maybe hours—of hope, followed by hope's opposite: fear and dread. It was the day the Italian armistice with the Allies was announced, followed by the German occupation. The landings of Allied ships south of Naples that night set off a ground war that would last twenty months. From this date on, Jewish Italians had to disappear underground—to hide, change identity, flee, do anything and everything to survive.

Late that night of September 8 and into the morning, the Allies' ships approached the Bay of Salerno, south of Naples. (They had landed in Sicily in July, and that set off another chain of events.) This time, as they came toward the coast, soldiers heard news of Italy's armistice with the Allies. There was discussion on the deck. Would the Italians they encountered be friendly, or were they still the enemy? And what about the Germans? Where were they? The soldiers speculated about what they could encounter as their boats approached the length of the Bay of Salerno.

The soldiers saw the beaches. *It was moonlit. As you go into Paestum itself,* combat engineer David Resnik said in an interview, *you hit the beaches and you hit the town and you see the mountains. You see ruins; you're amazed. You know they're ruins; you think they're Italian, maybe Greek. What are they doing here? How do we get through them? And then it all happens.*

German artillery, mines, bombs.

The Germans had anticipated their Italian allies might turn once they had deposed Mussolini, six weeks before, on July 25, and so they had built up troops and equipment throughout the peninsula. They were waiting. They defended mountainous fortresses, inland from the coast. They destroyed bridges, tunnels, culverts—anything that allowed the Allies to move. The combat engineer's job was to clear mines and rebuild roads and bridges, to make a way for the Allies to move ahead. A column of Allies moved up the eastern side of the country too.

Starting on September 8, Germans occupied north of the line of combat. On October 1, Allies arrived in Naples. There, Germans had battled a fierce and deadly local uprising and retreated in anticipation of the advancing Allies. Although that uprising and the imminent arrival of Allied troops might have successfully thwarted Germany's plan for the first major deportation of Jews from Italy, they were already working on their plan for Rome.

And so it was that as of September of 1943, Jews living in Italy north of the line of combat witnessed a deadly race, between the Allies moving up the peninsula and the Nazi deportation machine. The Final Solution was in full operation and Jewish Italians would be deported to Auschwitz-Birkenau.

The king and prime minster fled to the south of Italy, which was under control of the Allies. Italian soldiers had no orders. In her book *Salvarsi* (or *To Save Oneself*), Liliana Picciotto discusses the Resistance that erupted at this time. There had been resistance before, surely, but this mass resistance was new. Soon, in the hills and in the cities, men and women in partisan formations were doing whatever they could to impede the Germans and Fascists, to assist in the liberation of their country. Former soldiers also, now fleeing the Germans, were a part of it.

The battle in Italy was not only on the ground. Allied bombardments had rained down on cities since days after Italy joined the war on the side of Germany, in 1940. City dwellers fled their homes for the safer countryside. And the bombing continued after the armistice.

So that race was on, and the movement of the Allies was slowed greatly by a topography that favored defense, and defense was the Germans.

The Allies made another landing at Anzio four months later. It was so treacherous and bloody that at one point everyone—cooks, engineers, mechanics—was put on the line. *Sunny Italy*, they would jeer, as they walked in the cold rain and mud. In June of 1944, the Allies entered Rome.

But by the time the Germans retreated from Rome, they had deported more than one thousand Jewish Italians from that city to Auschwitz-Birkenau.

Two months after the Allies liberated Rome, but eight months before the liberation of Italy, from the tiny Italian island possession of Rhodes, off the coast of Turkey, 1,800 Jews were deported to Auschwitz-Birkenau. In all, 8,500 of the 39,000 Jewish Italians were deported, most of them to Auschwitz-Birkenau.

But there is no single date when the Italian Holocaust began. Starting this story in 1943 creates an arbitrary line between the before and after. It implies the story begins there. Of course, this epoch begins much earlier. We might say 1922, with the naming of Mussolini as prime minister, or three years later, with the establishment of the dictatorship. Mussolini's colonial war marks the beginning of explicitly racist policy, and then there was his alliance with the Germans in 1936. In 1938, the Racial Laws marked the expression of the explicit anti-Semitism of the regime. Or it might be on the day of chaos and reckoning, September 8, 1943. Or later that year, when loyal followers of Mussolini and collaborators with the Germans named Jews the enemy. The line could be drawn in any number of places. It might be necessary to go back to the creation of the ghetto in Rome, by Pope Paul, in 1555, or to the teachings of the Catholic Church, which helped to instill distrust toward the Jews. Of course, we could also say it began after the First World War. "It is disillusioned soldiers who overthrow a regime," Ernest Hemingway wrote, in one of his dispatches from Europe between the wars. We could begin then in 1919, with the first meeting of the Fascists in Milan. Surely, we might see these dates as symbols, and we consider them to try to understand. But, says Shoah memorial architect Guido Morpurgo, "The Shoah is not resolved."

Memory

The Allies liberated Rome in June of 1944, and then pushed on north up the peninsula. The country north of Rome was still at war, still occupied by the Germans.

Meanwhile, the Romans picked up their lives. They did not know the fates of those who had been taken from their homes, loaded into trucks and then train cars. They had seen violence, but the "radicality of the Shoah" was not yet known, the terrible secret not yet revealed.

Soon after the liberation of Rome, historian Liliana Picciotto writes, a committee was set up to do research to find the lost ones, those who had been deported from Rome. The Committee for the Research on Deported Jews (CRDE) would work with civil, military, political, and private organizations toward this end, as well as helping the families of the deported. Family members brought photographs of their loved ones to this committee, believing they were somewhere and might be found. The head of the Committee was Colonel Massimo Adolfo Vitale.

It happened elsewhere in Europe too. Images were "plastered at the gathering and information center in Paris, at Hotel Lutaetia," Picciotto writes, the general area for finding the lost ones, and for care and help to those reentering after deportation.

In Rome, in 1944, the photographs were collected and filed with "thin blue strips of leather stapled on, each one with a letter of the alphabet." Cards with names were handwritten and filed along with other identifying documents.

Many of the inquires came from family and friends of those who had been taken from their homes on October 16, 1943.

Eventually, after the war, the CRDE's mission was changed by the radical facts. Seventeen of those deported on October 16, 1943, survived. The others were killed at Auschwitz-Birkenau.

Colonel Vitale contributed the photos and documents collected by the CRDE to another group beginning to gather evidence for the historical record. These photos and documents would become the foundation of the Contemporary Jewish Documentation Center, or CDEC, located in Venice and later moving to Milan. Thousands of pieces of paper, photos, letters, journals, and newspaper accounts followed. Over time, historians and other staff—there were eventually staff—video-recorded hundreds of interviews, made films, and set up a *videoteca* for the films of others. CDEC is the main center for research on the Shoah and contemporary Judaism in Italy.

In fact, another small collection of photos, along with that of the CRDE, contains the primary photographic records Picciotto identifies in all of Italy that point to the Shoah.

That other small cache of photos, which is archived at the Museum of the Risorgimento, is an album of photos, eleven of which make a "very disquieting sequence." These pictures document "a police anti-Jewish action: concentrating on a garden of a villa of 20 or so people (three photographs), the truckload of German police (six photographs), portraits of erect soldiers following with their gaze the truck going away from them (two photographs). The photographer is unknown."

And herein Picciotto looks beyond the facts, at clues:

> But from where does the Shoah emerge in these 11 photos? One sees the Shoah in the resigned and frightened appearance of the Jews gathered in front of the German soldiers first put in line and then forced into a truck. Of the comportment of the two groups emerges all the violence of the episode. One, a group in street clothes, gathered like a flock, and the other, soldiers with guns pointed. Now, we know what happened to these people and so we know what these photos represent.
>
> They have intrinsic power, just as do the photos of loved ones that were gathered in Rome, pictures of children at a beach, families posed for a portrait, newlyweds bashful and hopeful. These normal,

everyday photos become our point of entry, which is our empathy. In the scenes of their ordinary lives, the highpoints of their ordinary lives, we can see ourselves.

Most of the people in the photos did not return. Most were killed on arrival at Auschwitz. Therefore, the task of people like Liliana Picciotto and others was to document that part of the story—the destruction—but also to listen to those who survived.

By now, many survivors have told their stories, not because it was pleasant to do so. To tell it again and again meant reliving trauma. They told it so that we would know, with hope that it would be known and that it might also be useful.

And so, we read articles and books, and attend events that commemorate the Shoah. And by learning, we hope to recognize what happened and possibly, for some of us, we hope to identify that terrible thread of tyranny and hate that continues to run through the woven consciousness of the world, appearing in this country or that country, including our own country.

Introduction

The people whose stories you find in this book lived through exceptional times and unimaginable circumstances. They suffered profound hardships under Mussolini's Racial Laws and then, five years later, saw their very lives attacked during the German occupation. After September 8, 1943, with their families, they were forced to hide, some changing their identities, and others crossing safely into Switzerland. They had become an enemy in their own country.

That each of these people agreed to meet with me continues to astound me these many years later. I met with one person after another, sat in their living rooms, asking them to share their experiences with me. Their generosity still shines as a bright star in my life.

And then there are the keepers of memory in Italy. The historians, archivists, an architect. They devote their lives to research, documentation, safekeeping, and public archiving so people like you and me can learn, so our children and grandchildren can learn. They were generous too.

Soon after beginning this project, a few people recommended that I visit an important archive in Milan. There, I began to meet these keepers of memory. This small group in Italy keeps the memory, investigates it, tells it. They are memory's hope. Why do they devote their lives to the collection and safekeeping of the stories of this epoch? You will learn about a few of them here, too.

The people I met changed the course of my life. As each year passed, the effects were almost imperceptible, but looking back now, as I send this book out, I see that I am a different person, professionally and in my personal life. Part of this change might have happened anyway, but some is mostly and inarguably a result of my attention to these stories shared with me by the people who you, too, will come to know.

As a result of listening to accounts told about that period of time, I am also more aware of certain trends in the politics of this current era. This project began before September 11, 2001, the date Americans were awakened by shattering news. On September 12, I was in a meeting with a room full of high school students from Gubbio, Italy, and Lenox, Massachusetts. Our task was to prepare for an interview with a Jewish Italian woman who had lived through the war. Our meeting—an account of it is included—provided one side of a frame for this project. The students' concerns that day, the questions they wanted to ask Maria Perla Ajo, signaled that we would be living through a period of unsettlement while learning about the 1930s and 1940s. One student wondered aloud if "today"—September 12, 2001—might be the beginning of the Third World War. Another wanted to know if living through the war had made Signora Ajo look at life with new eyes.

Now, in 2023, Signora Ajo's words still reverberate in my daily life. One piece of advice to the students was this: "Don't let tyranny happen, because it takes victims, blood, and years to rid your country of it."

A few people recommended that I include my own experiences of learning in the book. Marc Jaffe, the editor who helped me put it into a shape, who coaxed out the stories, convinced me to write more about myself. I was not inclined to do this. Who was I, after all, to include my story? How was it important? But I trusted that Marc and others might understand something that I did not grasp. I decided to chronicle my experience of meeting people, including the contexts in which I met them.

Then two events happened to help me decide to publish the book. (The book never seemed ready.)

First, on December 19, 2020, Nedo Fiano, a survivor of Auschwitz devoted to speaking about his experience, died. I wrote to express my condolences to historian Liliana Picciotto, who knew him well. She responded by telling me about his dedication to this memory and she ended her emailed message saying that I was now a part of a group responsible to tell this story.

Then, on June 15, 2022, the Shoah Memorial at Milan's Central Station was inaugurated. A friend, Jamie Keller, who appears as an ally early in this book, and I attended the public ceremony. We wanted to be there, feet on the ground, two of the many counted, celebrating this architectural and social achievement.

During the inaugural events, the architect, Guido Morpurgo, gave a talk. Looking from the entrance of the memorial, which lies deep in a remote part of the station, toward the glass-walled library—and that is another important story—he said: Books taken all together are bricks in the building of memory.

Finally, I should say that the details of stories as told to me are left intact, that is, place and family names, incidents, etc., relayed by the people who lived during Fascism and the war are written as they were told to me. If one of the accounts seemed to be out of sync with a known fact, I made a note of it in the text. Their accounts here are about their lives as told by them.

May this book be a small building block of memory.

— Judith Monachina, October 15, 2023

Part One: The Way In

Rinaldo Ribezzi

"I have nothing to tell you but memories," the priest said of his time during the war, before hanging up the phone.

A few days later, inside the church rectory, in a square cool room with bookcases, black-painted and plain oak furniture, the place was still. A single picture window brought in spare light and a view of the church across the street. Along one wall stood a long narrow table with a framed horizontal black-and-white photograph of a group of young men dressed in suits.

The sound of the priest's shoes on the hallway's tile floor disturbed the quiet. When Father Rinaldo Ribezzi entered the room, he sat in the chair at an angle to mine. He talked quickly in a voice that seemed to come from behind his palate, an organlike hum. He was thin and slightly stooped, probably not as tall as he had been, a young man out of seminary, and headed for a parish in America to work as a missionary. There were still enough native Italians to need him here. Instead, because of the war, he was sent to Santa Croce al Flaminio in Rome.

The timing of his assignment to Rome assured that his work there would not be ordinary. He was born shortly before the so-called March on Rome, an organized mobilization of Fascists, in 1922. Instead of repelling the armed Fascists with his army, King Vittorio Emanuele III asked Benito Mussolini, their leader waiting at a distance from Rome, to form a government. Within three years, Mussolini had transformed his country from a constitutional monarchy with a parliament to a dictatorship.

A few facts to put Father Ribezzi's life in a context. Fascism was thuggish and dictatorial, but, at first, it was not involved in the discrimination against Jews. By 1933, when the Fascist international diplomatic strategy began to change, this too began to change. By 1936, an intensive anti-Semitic media campaign was launched, and in 1938, Racial Laws targeting Jews were passed. In 1940, Italy joined the war on the side of the Germans. Immediately, the Allies—the British at this point—bombed Milan and other Italian cities. In July of 1943, the same month Allies landed in Sicily, Mussolini was removed from power and imprisoned by his government. Six weeks later came the day of great reckoning. The new government had signed a secret armistice with the Allies. Germans, already anticipating this might happen, built up troops inside Italy. And, as soon as the armistice became public, on September 8, they occupied much of the country. Father Ribezzi was there for the German occupation and for the complete chaos that followed.

His church hid refugees. Some of them were Jews who knocked on the door. "We already had young men," he said, soldiers who had decided not to fight alongside the German occupiers and Fascists at the onset of the occupation. Other churches in Rome were doing the same thing—harboring Jewish families and young men. Even nuns' cloisters had men and families in them, he said. He shared matter-of-factly about the steps he had taken in meeting the needs of the refugees: getting bedding, food, and books. He implied: this is what you do in these situations. He told me that one hundred people found refuge in the church's buildings on Via Guido Reni.

As I was leaving the rectory, Father Ribezzi held open the door to the street. "Are you Catholic?" he asked. I was surprised by the question. I was a reporter, and this was not a personal visit. My father was Catholic and my mother an Episcopalian, and their tendencies were ecumenical. I did not feel I belonged anywhere. I was in my late thirties at the time of this first visit with Father Ribezzi, and completely unreligious. How should I tell that to a priest?

"Read the Book of Tobit," he suggested. Intrigued by the assignment, I drove home, and pulled down a bible from my shelf. I had a few of them, different versions, that I kept with other religious and similar books of other traditions. I sat on my front porch, opened the bible, and read.

Tobit, the man for whom the book is named, is heroic, a good man. He does thankless work, such as burying the dead that have been thrown outside the city's walls. But then he is stricken with illness, becomes blind, sick, and discouraged. He asks God to take him from this life, and he decides to get his affairs in order just in case his request is heard. He directs his son, Tobiah, to take a journey to Nineveh to retrieve money from a relative. The journey will take Tobiah over dangerous roads, so Tobit hires a travel companion for his son, and the two young men set out. During the journey, Tobiah accomplishes much more than the retrieval of cash. He finds his bride, heals her from a horrible affliction, and, upon return home, heals his blind father. The hired companion is an angel, Tobiah learns, who has helped him accomplish all of this.

The book of Tobit is part of the Apocrypha, a body of writing considered sacred by Catholics, but not by Protestants or Jews. I would not have found it in every bible. As I sat on my porch in Great Barrington, Massachusetts, reading, I wondered if Father Ribezzi thought I might be on a special journey of some kind. The June day was mild, and as I thought about the story and the assignment, the word *grace* came to me. Many interviews are inspiring, but this one, with the priest, even though a bit cryptic, even incomplete, seemed like an opening to something larger. His courage—or what I perceived to be courage—stuck with me, and the sensation, and the word *grace*, came as a surprise.

As a reporter in the late 1990s, I interviewed local Holocaust survivors who wrote books and were giving talks. I wrote stories about a group of American adult children of survivors and German children of perpetrators, working together to heal. I learned of one family's exodus from Berlin, after Kristallnacht, and their immigration to Paris, where they sought help from one person who knew another. The family went from one house to the next looking for assistance with settling into Paris, including finding work. Their hosts in each house were polite but said they had nothing to offer. Eventually, the family was identified as enemy alien and sent to a labor camp run by the collaborationist Vichy government. Hearing this story, it occurred to me that the Holocaust, associated with brutal arrest and transport to death camps, began also in people's living rooms, with those first denials of support.

At a synagogue, author Daniel Goldhagen gave a lecture about his book *Hitler's Willing Executioners*. During the Q&A,

someone in the audience asked if there had been countries that had been less horrible for Jews than Germany or Poland. Goldhagen mentioned Italy as a place where Jews might have fared slightly better than the rest of the occupied countries. But the Italians, to whom I was related on my father's side, had been, after all, allies of Germany. And so, in part of my mind, deep inside and still untouched, I held a quiet burden. Who were the adoring people in the squares when Mussolini jutted his chin and talked of glory? How does something like this happen?

Burdens hidden quietly inside the nebulae of the mind remain there. Then one day, something happens to reveal them—in my case, it was the Goldhagen talk. And that was when I found Father Ribezzi. After meeting with him, I turned my attention to learning about the Holocaust in Italy, entering through the doorway of his story.

My knowledge was thin and had immense holes. By good fortune, Rabbi Robert Sternberg, who ran the Hatikvah Holocaust Education Center in nearby Springfield, Massachusetts, recommended books for me. He gave a weekend workshop for teachers on the Holocaust, and I took it, along with a Latin teacher who led a high school student exchange to Italy, and a few others. The Latin teacher, Jamie Keller, was a fellow student in my Italian class. I continued working at my job at the newspaper, of course.

About one year after our first interview, I tried to reach Father Ribezzi and learned he was no longer in Pittsfield. He had moved into a nursing home one hour away. Each time I visited him there—three times in all—he asked what I did for a living. He was losing his memory. The distant past was clear, but yesterday was forgotten. In one of our conversations at the nursing home, he recalled how a major church in Rome had been bombed, and there was news on the street that the quarter in which he lived would be next. His congregation raised prayers to Mary. When he told me the story, he cried "Mother!" as if still seeking her intervention.

During one of my visits, he found a little box in his room and took out photographs. He showed me one of a statue he had erected at another church, in Waltham, Massachusetts. It depicted the young Joseph and Mary with bowed heads before a rabbi who was marrying them. He wanted to tell the story of the couple as Jewish. He then passed me a cup of cranberry juice and dipped a cracker in his own cup, demonstrating his ritual.

Listening to Father Ribezzi's memories was like standing in front of a pond and noticing the reflection of the trees and sky on the still water's surface. Just when the scene comes into focus, someone throws a stone into the water and the image breaks up. Eventually the surface stills again; then there is a wind. That was when I took the first trip to Rome, to look for other parts of the story.

Rome, 2000

THE AVENTINO NEIGHBORHOOD had the luxury of quiet, the rush just beyond the hush of walls and sleek apartment buildings, cypress trees, granite and travertine, pale painted stucco and cement, beige and creamy peach, balconies with glass doors into private spaces. This residential area was a beautiful, even picturesque, retreat from the touristed city. Nearby, the 12 BCE pyramid tomb of Gaius Cestius pops up alongside a busy thoroughfare. A sullen young monk smoked as he leaned against a column in the courtyard of Sant'Anselmo. Two young Japanese women, dressed identically, sat on a bench, staring out at the wide empty field of the Circus Maximus, the immense Roman stadium, now a park where people run and walk their dogs.

On Via Marmorata, a billboard condemned the candidacy of Jorg Haider, a right-wing candidate in Austria. A few blocks away, a black swastika sprayed on a long stucco wall, in capital letters, announced the presence of SKINHEADS. I saw another graffito later that day: *Onore al Duce*, it said. As I took pictures of the billboard and graffiti, an uneasy feeling rose up. I wanted to be comfortable here, which meant inconspicuous, and documenting the graffiti, photographing from all angles, zeroing in on a target and stalking it, suddenly I was an actor, visible.

Before the trip I thought my project was about history, but the history I found was not a compartmentalized, packed-away past. Strains of memory very different from the one I was looking for were still being cultivated. It is one thing to know neo-Nazis exist, but it is a whole other to see proof of them through writing on the front wall of a peach stucco apartment building.

I had five days in Rome and only one appointment, at Father Ribezzi's wartime church. The main synagogue was open for limited tours, which included a history lesson about Roman Jewry for a small group of English-speaking tourists in the front of the sanctuary, then a walk through the museum. Jews first arrived in Rome about 2,200 years ago, during the time of the Maccabees. This synagogue was built after the institution of the national state, in 1870. Its square dome can be seen from a great distance. Inside and under glass, we saw intricately stitched silk thread on linen, in deep reds, golds, and blues, ritual parochot and mappot—the curtain that covers the ark and Torah, and the cloth that swaddles the Torah scroll. The textiles come from the ancient five synagogues that were replaced by this one.

The visit to the synagogue and the tour of the museum grounded all my subsequent learning in this reality—Jewish history here was ancient.

The next day, across the river from the synagogue, in the library of the Union of the Italian Jewish Communities (UCEI), a young woman graciously retrieved books.

Liliana Picciotto, the historian affiliated with the Contemporary Jewish Documentation Center (CDEC) in Milan, had written one of the books. I did not know that I would eventually meet her, or how important she was as a keeper of memory. In my notebook, I wrote down numbers: 8,500 Jews deported from Italy to concentration camps during the German occupation, approximately 39,000 Jews in Italy at the start of the war. (I later learned that the numbers were uncertain at the time of the writing of her book, and the long process of cross-checking was still happening as I read that afternoon.)

On the last day, at Santa Croce in Via Flaminia, Father Ribezzi's wartime church, I passed a statue of Mary. It had been placed there to thank her for her help during the war, Father Ribezzi had said.

In the church office, I sat with the pastor who faced his computer searching a list of items in the archive. He knew nothing about what had happened there during the war, but he found a book about the pastor of the church from that period. In it, a few pages covered the church's activities with refugees, and in these pages, Father Ribezzi was mentioned. The pastor had invited an interpreter to join us, Jose Paul Koovanil, an Indian seminary student in residence, and, afterwards, Jose took the tram and train with me as far as his university. The Catholic Church had educated him from the time he was a young boy in Kerala, a state on India's Malabar Coast, and now he was studying to be a priest. He spoke several languages, including Hebrew, Latin, and Greek, and was doing his dissertation on ethics and the Human Genome Project. In our conversation, I learned more about Jose than I did about the church, but somehow, even though little was revealed, I went back to my guest-house room feeling content. In my notebook, I wrote that Jose had offered to interpret other meetings for me.

If Father Ribezzi had kept his memory a little longer, his story would have become an article, and I might have stopped there. Instead, he opened a door to my curiosity and then he went away, and with him his story. At the time, I knew so little about memory or Holocaust research in Italy that I went with notebook and pen, and eventually, with a tape recorder, to talk with people: a rabbi, a child of a survivor, a survivor, a scholar. One meeting led to another, one referral to another. This project had been circling around me, appearing as an interest, and resulting in numerous articles about survivors. Father Ribezzi's story gave me a way in, an entry that invited me to deepen my understanding. Certainly, there were others I could meet.

Rome, 2001

Jews have lived in Rome since 161 BCE. During the period of papal rule in the central swath of Italy, including Rome, their fates rose and fell, as in all of Europe. Then, in 1555, Pope Paul IV's papal bull, a public decree, established the Roman Ghetto, a trapezoidal area along the Tiber. The space inside became the enforced home of Rome's two thousand Jews; separating them meant there would be no more "contamination" of Christian ways. Jews returned to the enclosure every evening, two hours after dusk.

Jamie Keller, the fellow student in my Italian class in Massachusetts, had invited me to accompany a group of high school exchange students to Rome and help her add an Italian Jewish history lesson to the already full itinerary. We started with this lesson about the papal bull and a tour of the Ghetto.

Jamie, who is Jewish, and I knew that Jews had long been subject to regular persecution. But our knowledge was uneven. During the Crusades, the Church was going after Muslims in the Holy land, but historian Cecil Roth noted, "Once religious passions are aroused, it is always difficult to restrict them to one channel." By the end of the Third Crusade, Jews in the Rhine Valley, France, and England had suffered expulsions and massacres. Then, in 1492, in her Catholic Reconquista, Spain's Queen Isabella ordered Jews to leave; the same edict followed in Portugal, and then in the Spanish territory of Sicily. Sixty years later, the pope established the Roman Ghetto.

(Historian Sara Buda later pointed out that the expulsions and the creation of the ghettoes "were two options for a similar question. In a Catholic world that was striving to renovate itself," she said, "the Pope chose not to expel Jews outside the country, but rather to build ghettoes.")

Our guide that day, a petite nun, dressed in corduroy skirt and Oxford blouse, delivered the lesson to the fifteen jetlagged American students at her office on Via Plebiscito. This tour of the Ghetto was listed in a popular guidebook, and it came as a surprise that nuns organized it. The nun's organization, the International Christian-Jewish Documentation Center (SIDIC), was founded in 1971, after the Second Vatican Council. In one of many coincidences that marked the early days of this project, Sister Marguerite McGrath and Rabbi Robert Sternberg (director of Hatikvah Holocaust Education Center, in Massachusetts) knew each other. The two had collaborated on tolerance education.

That day, with the students, Sister Marguerite explained that the affiliated Sisters of Sion had taken a role in Christian Jewish relations because they realized church teachings had been destructive to Jews. Pleased that her guests were students of Latin, Sister Marguerite made a copy of the papal bull, *cum nimis absurdum*, for later reading. Then she waved us all out and down the stairs for a tour of the Ghetto.

It was morning, and the city was busy with people getting to work. Winding through the maze of narrow streets, the students, still half asleep, knit caps covering their heads, perked up at graffiti written along walls we passed. They asked her about its significance—anarchy was one of the symbols—and posed for pictures in front of it.

But at Portico d'Ottavia, built by Emperor Augustus in 27 BCE, and named for his sister, Sister Marguerite began to peel back older layers. Now, that ancient arched doorway and columns stand at the end of a busy street with popular cafes and restaurants. She showed us how engineers had built upon the existing flood-prone area, now partially excavated.

Called an enclosure, the Ghetto grew in size and changed over various papal reigns, and altogether disappeared (as an enforced residence) a few times. Its permanent elimination was one of the fine moments in the conquest of Rome in 1870, after the last battle in the fight for unification of Italy, when the French troops defending the Pope had to withdraw to fight the Prussians elsewhere. Then the Italian troops defeated the Papal Army.

The end of papal rule in Central Italy came after a long period of battle toward Italy's unification, waves of uprising to eliminate foreign domination in the southern and northern regions, and papal rule in the middle. Jewish Italians were very active in the new army, fighting for a nation in which they wanted to live as equals. Called the Risorgimento, the unification came with dramatic changes for the Vatican. With the final battle, in Rome, the Holy See lost its place of power and its sense of dominion, its temporal rule. Though the church continues to wield power internationally and nationally, the government of the entire Italian peninsula has been secular since 1870.

By the Second World War, Jews had served at the highest levels of government, including as prime minister, and intermarriage was common. But many Jews still lived in this neighborhood—approximately 8,000 in the city overall—when the Germans occupied Rome on September 9, 1943. One month later, before dawn on October 16, 1943, German officers surrounded and blocked the very street where we stood as well as other streets in various neighborhoods, Sister Marguerite told the students, who were now alert. They fired shots and began banging on doors, arresting Jewish families, old people, children. With guns raised, they pulled people out of their homes. They cut telephone lines, and they pushed their prisoners through the same street where we now stood and into waiting trucks. 1,259 people were arrested that day and brought to a nearby military academy, where some were eventually released. Two days later, 1,220 people were directly deported to Auschwitz. Of those, 17 people survived. No church official was present of course, but their hands were not clean. Centuries of church teachings about Jews had contributed to this genocide.

The students, standing in a huddle, looked at the ground as they listened. To stand in this ancient but otherwise ordinary street, to hear that history in that spot, gave us all a moment to inhabit the place differently, consciously. We all stood together in silence.

Maria Perla Ajo

Over a span of three days, Jamie led the group to Roman sites, including St. Peter's Basilica and the Sistine Chapel, the Colosseum, and the Forum. We walked everywhere, often along the long river roadway, with its tree roots disrupting the sidewalks. Then, the group boarded a train for the school exchange in Gubbio. As our train slid out of Rome's Termini station and climbed into the Umbrian hills, all talk slowed down, and eventually the students and leaders were quiet again. The train ride gave room to lay out our thoughts, to absorb or reflect on our memories of Rome, and to sleep. The high school teachers knew to keep their students very busy, to tire them out and avoid mischief. Jamie took the students to Rome first, on each exchange visit, because they would be less confident in the first days of the trip and therefore less apt to get into trouble there. In Gubbio, a smaller place, with several hosts helping to watch out for the students, the risks were lower. Her method worked: on the train, everyone was tired.

In Gubbio, students went off with their host families. As was tradition for this exchange, each morning the group met at the school for an excursion: to Florence, or nearby Spello, or Assisi. One day, we arrived at the school and were led into the auditorium. It turned out that the teachers had scheduled an event, and we would be a part of it. We thought our Italian Jewish history lesson was over, but we soon learned that the other participants, panelists, included a Jewish woman who was a teenager during the war, Maria Perla Ajo. We learned that we would be on a panel as well, to share about our visit to the Roman Ghetto and the Lenox Gubbio Exchange.

Signora Ajo and I sat at opposite ends of the long table, in front of an audience of a couple hundred students and their teachers, most of whom were from Gubbio, along with the small group from Lenox. As a history professor spoke, I happened to sit back in my chair and look to my right. Signora Ajo was looking in my direction, as though waiting for me to turn and notice her. She closed her eyes and lowered her head. When she opened them, they were still looking at me. There was the trace of a smile in them, or was it a question?

Then, from her father's diary, which he had kept during the German occupation, she read a passage about her mother:

> Contemptuous of the danger, completely intent on the care and protection of her children, precious and very affectionate comfort for my tribulations, which followed us everywhere: in the mountains, the winter, in the mud and snow; in the city full of serious and hidden threats. Here in Rome, she knocked at one hundred doors to be able to put her children in safe places.

In 1943, her family fled their home in Gubbio and made it to Rome by train. They changed their names and split up to hide in different places. They were Jewish, and the German occupation was already three months old.

She read several excerpts from the diary. Talks followed, by a history professor and, finally, a priest who had lived in the area during the war.

Then Vice Principal Corrado Baldoni closed the event with a statement, "The past only speaks to us according to that which we ask."

Later that evening, we, the American guests, sat at our host Giovanna Brunelli's round table enjoying the dinner she had made. In a dining alcove off the kitchen, we saw evidence of Giovanna's life: one painting of ringed planets on an oversized handmade sheet of paper hung on a white curving wall; a photo of an uncle, one of nieces, and other personal memorabilia on a tall case; and inside it, books—philosophy, history, literature. Behind us, two glass doors to the balcony showed as black rectangles—it had grown dark outside. By contrast, the space we occupied in the dining room, like our conversation, was warm, light, floating.

"Do you think Signora Ajo would be willing to talk with students about her own experience," I asked Giovanna. She had read from her father's diary, but perhaps we could hear her story. She had been a teenager, after all. Giovanna thought she might be interested.

Assisi

The following afternoon, we went to Assisi, where Mount Subasio's stone buildings meld cream and rose, and the medieval hill town seemed to glow. Students took a tour of the Basilica, in the process of restoration after the 1997 earthquake, and another teacher met me outside the church to bring me to meet a priest who had been involved in an underground movement during the German occupation. We climbed the narrow alleys, quiet beyond the gift shops and cafes, and after a few steep twists, arrived at a hilltop bookstore where we met Father Aldo Brunacci.

I knew almost nothing about Assisi or Saint Francis but had read *The Assisi Underground*, a nonfiction book about a group of priests and nuns who sheltered Jews there during the occupation. The book is the stuff of an adventure movie and was made into a film directed by its author, Alexander Ramati. In it, Father Rufino Niccacci secures secret hiding places for Jewish refugees to stay after the occupation, September 8, 1943; organizes the manufacture of false identification cards with printers in town; and speeds on bicycle between Umbrian hill towns to deliver false documents, enabling the refugees to live in the open with new names and identities. In the book, Niccacci is the key operative in this dangerous underground work, in which discovery by a German soldier could mean imprisonment or death.

Father Brunacci was waiting for us at the door. After greetings, we moved into a cool, almost dark study. As we sat, the priest quickly announced, "The book and film are absolutely false."

"Thousands of refugees were in Assisi," he told us. They were fleeing bombarded cities, avoiding conscription by the German military, or deportation. "Yes," he said, "there were convents involved, and Jews did find refuge here." Otherwise, the details of the book are incorrect, and in fact, he said he had been a major player in the underground. He had been the one on the bicycle, for example.

Father Brunacci presented a challenge to a popular narrative, a puzzle piece, which for me would likely remain a stray one among many. My own inquiry had just begun, with no clear direction or goal. This encounter did nothing to direct its course. Soon, someone else would provide a full view of Father Brunacci's story, but for now, my approach was to cast a wide net and observe the stories that landed in it.

Soon after returning home, I applied for a grant from the Olivetti Foundation—their entry in the Foundation Center's grant directory emphasized their support of cross-cultural projects such as the Lenox Gubbio Documentary Project, as we were calling it. I was surprised when, two months later, a check arrived. It would pay for travel and a filmmaker to teach students to video record our interview. Later I would set out to learn more about the Olivetti family and why this project might be of interest to them. But for now, I was simply grateful for the check. My modest salary at a community newspaper did not support travel. The grant paid for expenses, but it also felt like encouragement, and it bolstered my commitment to the project.

Maria Perla Ajo

ON SEPTEMBER 10, 2001, the Italian students arrived in Lenox for their exchange visit. They had already visited Washington, DC. Now, they would explore the Berkshires around Lenox, in Massachusetts, and take day trips to New York and Boston. They would stay with students' families and immerse themselves in the English language and American customs. But this time, there was a new element: students would prepare for their interview with Maria Perla Ajo, which they would conduct and record during the following winter, in Gubbio.

On the morning of September 11, the students and teachers took a bus to the Clark Art Institute to look at impressionist paintings. While there, Jamie, their teacher, received a call from her principal, who told her about what was happening in New York City and Washington, DC. The planes. The World Trade Center. The Pentagon.

That night, I called Jamie, their teacher, and suggested we cancel our meeting scheduled the next morning to prepare for the interview with Signora Ajo. Wouldn't the Second World War seem irrelevant, even obsolete? Jamie said no. "The students were upset. Some of them cried on the bus on the way back to Lenox." They were worried about getting home, about what might happen next. "A productive activity might help."

We gathered Wednesday morning to prepare for the interview. And the students proved me wrong. When asked to come up with questions they might ask Signora Ajo, they did not hesitate. *Did you wonder why it was happening? Did you think it would ever end? Does war make you look at life with new eyes? Is this the Third World War?*

Maria Perla Ajo

The filmmaker Tish Streeten, teacher Giovanna Brunelli, and I spent a week preparing with the students. A few days before the scheduled interview, Signora Ajo sent word through that she did not feel well. She did not know if she could meet with us.

I had made a mistake by not going to visit upon arrival in Gubbio. It was a simple gesture of courtesy and care. Perhaps she was anxious, and we could reassure her. Giovanna called to arrange a visit. Could she trust us with this story? Should she dig out and display memories from a traumatic time? She knew the Italian teachers, but she did not know me.

She wanted to meet with us to go over our plans, she said. We were teaching students how to conduct the interview, we explained, and through the interview they would learn the history from someone who had lived it. We left her house unsure of her decision.

The next day, Signora Ajo was feeling better. We could go to her home, as planned.

On the day of our interview, Signora Ajo opened her apartment door and the students floated over to a window to see the red tiled roofs of their city. The student camera crew got ready. The rest of the group selected seats around the living room, in chairs and on the floor. The students held sheets of paper with questions.

We had spent a week preparing for this interview, and they were suddenly shy, on the edge of learning. Signora Ajo spoke to the students about her family. Her parents had met and married during the years that Mussolini was transforming the country to a dictatorship. Though Fascism may have been racist, as evidenced by the colonial wars in the 1930s, Mussolini had earlier scoffed at Hitler's anti-Semitic obsession. And in fact, some Jews also belonged to the Fascist party. Signs began to portend a change: In 1934, the arrest of a group in Turin marked early propaganda of Jews as antifascists and instigators. Then, in 1936, he established a relentless anti-Semitic media campaign, with the state-controlled media. In September of 1938, the first of the Racial Laws were passed by the Senate. Over the next several months, the laws were expanded, eventually creating a citizenship of second class. That year, Maria Perla Ajo was a young teen. The new laws forbade Jewish children from attending public schools. Eventually Jews were forbidden from owning businesses with more than one hundred employees. Jewish professionals were severely limited in the practice of their work and Jews were ejected from social organizations, the military, and public service.

"In Gubbio, we felt it less," Maria Perla said. Hers was one of only a few Jewish families in town. Other lawyers invited her father to work under their signature. But eventually, in court, "he had so many sticks poked in his wheels that he gave up his practice."

Signora Ajo talked in summaries, perhaps because she was young when it happened. Like passengers in a car along a new route, but not the driver of the car, the teens were not the ones making the decisions; they were not navigating. They were affected, but differently from their parents, who had to make a living, protect their children.

Maria Perla Ajo, a young girl, left. The photo of a photo was taken by students from the Istituto Tecnico Sperimentale, Gubbio, 2002

"Then there were the famous Racial Laws," she said. "You can't do this; you can't do that."

"My father had made a mixed marriage, and all four of us were baptized and brought up according to Catholicism. But later on, they turned the page: mixed marriages and promises of being Catholic did not matter. 'You are called Ajo, you are Jewish, and good night.'"

The police often interrogated her family's maid, to learn about any anti-Fascist conversations in the family, but despite the new law, it seemed from her story that they were able to keep the maid. The new laws forbade so-called Aryan household help in Jewish homes. There were lots of parades, and uniforms were required every time a visiting Fascist bigwig arrived in town, she said. "Those who said bad things about Fascism spoke in secret, and others were speaking everywhere." In speaking against Fascism they might be taking a great risk.

Italy declared war against France and England in 1940. It seemed to Mussolini that Germany had already won, so he joined on the side of Hitler. Allies, the British at this point, immediately began to bomb Italian cities. To escape the bombings, city dwellers left their homes for the countryside. Gubbio, however, was not an industrial city or on important train lines. While Allies bombed Milan and other cities, rail lines, and industrial sites, Gubbio remained relatively safe.

In July of 1943, Allies landed in Sicily and, on July 25, Mussolini was voted out of power by his own Grand Council. The next day, King Vittorio Emanuele III had him arrested and immediately imprisoned, and invited General Pietro Badoglio to take his place. At that point, Germans, understanding what might happen next, began to amass more troops in Italy and began the search for the secret prison of Mussolini. On September 8, 1943, American General Dwight D. Eisenhower announced the Italian armistice with the Allies. General Badoglio confirmed the news but gave little direction as to how Italians, in particular the military, should respond. The country was in chaos. Soldiers were fleeing conscription by the now occupying Germans and remaining Fascists. In fact, Badoglio and the king fled, escaping first by car and then by boat to the south of Italy, occupied by the Allied forces.

"Germans considered it a betrayal, and they began the real slaughter," Signora Ajo explained. "Here in Gubbio, immediately after the armistice, in Ponte d'Assi, their jeeps were already there, and tanks were ready to stop a defection of the Italian Army." In all, they deported more than six hundred thousand Italian military personnel to labor camps.

As the armistice was announced, Allied troops were already on ships approaching the Bay of Salerno, just south of Naples. After they disembarked, they began to cover ground, eventually pushing the Germans north. But it was a bloody battle, and it went very slowly. And so now, Italy was occupied by Germans in the north, and by the Allies in the south—in 1943, the Allies included the Americans. Allied air assaults continued hitting Italian cities as their armies slowly made their way up the peninsula.

After September 8, the Ajo family had to disappear like all Jewish families north of the Allied troops.

Maria Perla's father's diary recounts the agony of decision-making during this time. At first, the family stayed in a house they owned in the nearby countryside. Then, realizing that it was too obvious a place to hide, they asked others in neighboring country places, tiny villages like Ghigiano, Goregge; but these places were filled with other refugees. "Then, the good Ubaldo Vergari, he was happy to help us in this very sad time and made available two small rooms and a kitchenette attached to the house."

In Maria Perla's words: "And so we went to creep in, on top, among the mountains. The family stayed in a farmhouse with no water. The farmers had kindly given us a part of their house, and we managed the best we could. There were a lot of us: Dad, his brother, the two wives and six children, and so we were on top of each other, mattresses on the ground. Food could be found, more or less, because we were in the country. And we had the caretaker, the one of who took care of our vines [nearby], Sisto Ragni, who was more than a father, a brother to us. He would come on foot or however he could come from San Martino in Colle, to Sant'Andrea del Calciano, in order to bring us food and news."

Three months after their hiding began, Sisto came to them and said, "In Gubbio, everybody knows where you are."

These were lonely places in the mountains, and the Ajo family began to hear that Germans were searching for Jews. In his diary, he wrote of hearing about the roundup in Rome, where even a disabled old man had been thrown into a truck. To add to the terror, on December 1, 1943, he wrote about his wife hearing on the radio news that Italian Fascists declared Jews to be the enemy. They were now directed by their leadership to participate—they would now participate jointly with the Germans—in the arrest and deportation of Jews. It was no longer just the Germans, but Italians participating in the arrests. Fascist Italian police joined the Germans in the arrests.

The adults in the Ajo group decided that rather than go to another isolated place, they would go to Rome, where they had some friends. "We say, in the open sea, you can get lost more easily," Signora Ajo told us.

But that decision weighed heavily on her father: "I found myself confronting a pressing decision," he wrote. "The family wanted to go to Rome, but wouldn't it be better to find another mountain place?" However, with the others in favor of the decision to go to Rome, and without any time to debate it, he went along with them. "Could I take it upon myself, in this moment, to change course? To oppose a plan that had been embraced by the others? It being late, if we didn't board the train right away, we would not have time to take the train on which the others were traveling. We boarded the train."

Leaving on December 9, their group took four days to make the trip—the main train lines had been bombed. When they arrived in Piazzale Flaminio, more decisions had to be made. The uncle, also married to a non-Jew, had in-laws in Rome with whom his little family would hide.

Signora Ajo said, "My father phoned one of his dearest friends, who was Professor Benveduti, who said to him, 'Of course, come no problem.' But his house was small, and there he had his mother, another lady as a guest, four or five people could live there! And so, it happened that my uncle, whose daughters had been at the Assunzione Boarding House, got someone to phone the Mother Superior and they sent me and my sister there. And they, Dad and brother, the first thing they had to do was to get rid of all the nails under their shoes. Because we dressed like people who live in the mountains. They had nailed shoes and we had such boots, such socks! Because we had escaped with few things…so the first thing to prevent the ones living downstairs from hearing strange noises from the nailed shoes was to take the nails off the single pair of shoes we had. (Professor Benveduti, a Fascist, had a mixed record. Here, with the Ajo family, he was altruistic.)

"The boarding house was protected by the Vatican, and so they would send food. But only the Mother Superior knew that we weren't what we said we were. That is, we were using my mother's surname. So, the hardest part was to convince my sister not to tell the truth, that is, that she wasn't Paola Ajo but Paola Antonucci. At five years old, it is not easy. The others stayed at the Benvedutis'. My brother and my father never went out. They only moved around a little, at night.

"But my mother had false documents. Dad had a friend in Rome who got some documents from a little town called Monopoli, where the registrar's office had been destroyed. So, they couldn't be traced. They changed their names and personal details. All of them came from Monopoli. In Monopoli there wasn't a registrar's office anymore; all things considered, it wasn't easy to check up on them.

"We still had our friend Sisto, who even came to Rome to bring us food. To face the ongoing problem of food, though, my mother and a friend of the Benveduto family, who was also staying with them, from Sardinia, decided to make cakes and sell them. Clelia, who was a very good cook, could make a kind of Sardinian cake called casadinas, for which we could find the ingredients. Guess where they went and sold them? To the German headquarters in the Flora! We made real fools of them. We went and sold these cakes at the German headquarters. Mum had a false identity card, the other lady was beyond suspicion. Two ladies who wanted to make ends meet, make cakes and find the money to eat, weren't very suspicious. And they fed the German headquarters at the Flora with these cakes, and it was important for them, because it meant they could eat. When we went there on Sundays, they tried to pull a rabbit out of a hat for us. People ate roots, disgusting things."

"Were you frightened? What was it like to live in this way?" a student asked.

"The most tragic moment for our family was when one of my cousins got sick, a seventeen-year-old girl, staying in Burano with her parents. And she got leukemia. I mean, to get leukemia is something frightening and scary even now. Then it meant death for sure. From Burano, in secret, they took her to her grandmother's in Gubbio, and here [in Gubbio] she was treated by a certain Dr. Fabrini, who was the director of the hospital. He too was known as an anti-Fascist, and was bullied and watched, so he could not see her when necessary. But by night and in secret he took great risks to do the little he could. After a while, she died. The funeral was done in secret. If my uncle had gone in daylight he would have been caught. That was the hardest thing we had to bear. As for the rest, yes, fears, uneasiness, pains not from a physical but from a moral point of view."

"Did you feel hope that it would end?" another student asked.

"I must say there was hope, also, because there was this Radio London, which communicated with us. We were forbidden to listen to it, but many people listened. They told us where the Allies were. The way from Ostia took them such a long time, the landing in Anzio, it took long because it was so hard. But we knew that they were nearer and nearer, and that they would be here sooner or later."

The Allies did arrive, between June 4 and 5, 1944. (The official date is June 4.)

"We could hear them from far away. In the meantime, we could see the Germans escaping, and hear the rumble of their vehicles.

"The first jeeps we saw, I think we could have jumped out of the window to welcome them more enthusiastically. I remember we had gone to our friend's house, because we knew the Germans were leaving. They only worried about escaping themselves. We were on a terrace at Monteverde, at these friends' place, to wait for this arrival. We saw the American soldiers parading in Viale del Re. You were a real joy for us, your arrival," she said, looking at me. She paused and continued, "Because it was the end of a nightmare for us."

(After the war, the name of the street Viale del Re was changed to Via Trastevere.)

I pushed a slip of paper into a student's hand. She asked Signora Ajo what she would like us to learn.

"I would like you to understand that any dictatorship is like poison; that you don't accept other people's commands; that everyone can go on reasoning with his or her mind. I would like you to oppose the worst things you see around, so as to avoid that someone can rise again and get so much power that they walk all over other people. Since that can happen again in the blinking of an eye.

"Therefore, you must be careful, see the first signs of prevaricating, arrogance, or absolutism, and put a stop to them. Because the beginning is always similar, at the beginning everybody is nice, good, they want to be helpful for the country. 'There are things which are wrong, let's try to make them right, let's do something new!'" Though addressing the student who had asked the question, she looked directly at me again while speaking, as if to say, I would like this for you, too.

"Look I have no recipe," she continued. "I think it is right that you care about the problems of society, from the smallest society, which is school, to your local community, that above all you look at things also with critical eyes. The things you believe wrong, say them, because you must build your future yourselves. So, all the things which are wrong, at least speak as much as possible, speak aloud, yes, in order to avoid the moment when it's not possible to say them anymore. A dictatorship," she said, "takes victims, blood, and years to remove."

We had come to the end of the interview. She seemed relieved; a burden had lifted. She went to the kitchen and returned with a tray of sodas. We had brought flowers, and she placed them on the coffee table where we sat. Students took pictures of photos in her albums, for later use.

Already, I was thinking about the pronouns: "We made fools of them," she said of her mother and her friend when the two women sold casadinas to the German occupiers; the 'you" in "You were a joy to us." To her, and maybe to others, in particular, elders who remembered, I was a representative of a country, of America, the Allies. Even while traveling, an American represents her country, perhaps more so when working with a group of school students in an exchange. When Maria Perla looked at me, admonishing me to speak against tyranny, I became the American of today. The American of 2002, a world power, recently attacked by terrorists, that responded by initiating war in Afghanistan, and at the same time passing something called the Patriot Act, which could lie in wait to infringe on civil liberties. We were subjected to red and orange alerts, warnings of the likelihood of another attack. Fear was encouraged. Soon, we would have another war, justified by our leaders' false claims of weapons of mass destruction in Iraq: prevaricating. Eventually, years later, a president would try to stage a violent coup in our country. Signora Ajo's words still resonate.

Walking back into town, the students, Giovanna, Tish, and I passed through the Piazza of the 40 Martyrs, named for that massacre of forty people from Gubbio by German officers. The park is New England-like, with trees and walkways crossing from one end to the other. But a medieval loggia flanks it. Here weekly outdoor markets are held. After an interview like the one with Maria Perla Ajo, all landscape and landmarks, the loggia, with its arched, open porticoes, the nearby church, and even the trees seem more alive, even sentient. I wanted to ask them: What can you tell us?

Rome

ON THE WAY HOME, in Rome, I met Amos Luzzatto, the president of the Union of Jewish Communities (UCEI) at his office. It seemed that UCEI might be a place for referrals to people, for answers to questions.

Dr. Luzzatto's family had left Italy for Palestine soon after the implementation of the Racial Laws of 1938. The family returned after the war, but he did not talk about himself—I learned all this later. In fact, at first, he tutored me in contemporary Jewish Italian geography, in particular about Jews living in various cities. "In Milan, Florence, Turin, and Livorno, he said, Jews from Morocco and Tunisia have arrived since the war. Iranian, Libyan, and Egyptian Jews immigrated here, too." He lamented the fact that it was they and not the Italian Jews who tended to speak and read fluent Hebrew in the synagogue. At one point he asked if I had seen the main synagogue in Rome. "Did you notice it looks like a church?"

Dr. Luzzatto talked about UCEI and its work, representing Italian Jewry in every official situation, including Parliament.

He seemed to be subtly saying UCEI was not the place to discuss or learn about the war. He continued with Jewish Italian geography. Jews in Southern Italy were very few, he continued, for the same reason Spain lost its Jewry. Sicily and Naples were under Spanish rule at the time, in the 1490s, and the Spanish policy of conversion or expulsion drove people underground or away. Some people in Southern Italy are trying to go back to Judaism now, he told me. He seemed a bit suspicious of their motives.

Then he turned to the war. He recommended that I meet his historian son, Gadi Luzzatto, and interview his cousin, Virginia Gattegno, who had been deported to Auschwitz. She lived in Venice and occasionally spoke in schools. Speaking about the experience was extremely difficult for survivors, "but they look strong and sturdy and cry afterwards," he said. They do it because it is a duty.

"Yes, continue with your interviews," he concluded. "I believe everyone has been interviewed, but one never knows if a new way of telling the story may help people see it differently." He recommended a visit to the main archive, in Milan.

Leaving his office, I turned back and saw that he was watching me with a look of puzzlement or as if stepping outside of the scene to observe it. I left with that impression of him, and with an awareness of the generosity of people, it seemed, wherever I turned.

Graziella Viterbi

WHILE IN ROME, a friend of a friend from home introduced me to two of her friends, both Jewish Italian women who had lived here through the war.

It happened that after the first trip in February of 2001, a Lenox student wrote an article about the Lenox Gubbio exchange and the visit to the Roman Ghetto, and it ran in the newspaper I coedited. Dave Resnik, a neighbor, read the article and told us he had been in the United States Fifth Army in Italy during the war. Soon, Dave lent books, opened maps, and gave me the telephone number of a friend who lived in Rome and, who, in the 1950s, had married a Jewish Italian man.

Dave's friend Sally Castelnuovo lived on Via di Sant'Elena, near Largo di Torre Argentina, in a building owned by the family of her husband, Giorgio Castelnuovo. Giorgio had been kept from attending university because of the Racial Laws. During the occupation, his family hid at a dermatological hospital. Now Sally, an artist, a widow, still lived in the building on Via Sant'Elena, and her adult children had apartments there, too. In fact, Via Sant'Elena is around the corner from the ghetto, with its residential door facing the direction of that neighborhood and its commercial front facing the busy Via Arenula, very near Large di Torre Argentina, with its buses and trams. From her penthouse terrace the red rooftops of Rome spread out in every direction. We drank spicy tea and then bundled up in our winter coats.

It was midafternoon in January and already dim when we took the tram across the river to Sally's friend's house in the Trastevere neighborhood. There, in the apartment that had belonged to the family of Marina Della Seta since she was a child, we sipped hot tea surrounded by the brocade and long draperies of the spacious living room. In the warm cave of ambling rooms, slender Marina made and poured tea, coming and going from the room where we sat.

Another woman, Graziella Viterbi, arrived and took off her beret and heavy coat. She had a deep voice, and when she sat down, she quickly dove into her story. "When the Racial Laws were passed," she said, "I went for a walk in a wooded area and felt happy to be not one of them."

"Not one of them?" Marina asked what she meant.

"To not be the oppressor?" Sally asked.

"Yes," Graziella said, then elaborated. "I did not suffer from the persecution. I thought it was the most foolish thing possible. Members of my mother's family were later sent to the concentration camps, and for this I suffered. But for the persecution, absolutely not. I was happy to not be one of them."

"That's quite a moment you had," I said.

Graziella nodded, but Sally did not buy it. She was sure that Graziella must have been upset, must have asked why. Despite Graziella's assurances, Sally expressed her disbelief, from various angles. Finally, Marina, in her singing and almost tentative voice, convinced Sally by lowering it: "We had no time to ask why."

Graziella added: "Now you can ask why, but it's a question that nobody answered in the past and we will not answer in the future."

Sally surrendered.

The three women gave me a chance to look at it, too. Sally, the American, asked why, and could not understand how what seemed a natural adolescent question, why or why me, had not occupied her two friends, both of whom had lived at roughly the same time as she, but were actually in the war. For the first time, I understood: Everything was imminent. How can anyone who has not lived through such urgency understand it? Sally and I could not understand, but we would both, in our own way, try, and because we sat with them and heard their voices as they told their stories, we felt their certainty.

That day, Graziella wondered why I would bother to write another book. "Nobody is interested," she said. She went into schools to tell her story and saw firsthand that people were not interested in the history. She did it anyway, she said, because it was important to her to pass on her particular story, her memory of the events.

Graziella's family, her parents and her younger sister Miriam, had lived in a palazzo on the portico leading to the cathedral in Padua. "In Padua, I remember they burned our synagogue. I remember I saw the synagogue fire. We had many men beaten in the night. We were always afraid for the fathers. In Padua, we had intimidating phone calls in the late evenings. In fact, I hate telephones still." Just a girl, frightened about what was happening outside, in her city, Graziella started to close the shutters at dusk.

In September of 1943, she was seventeen years old. Her family was on vacation in the mountains when they learned that the Italians had surrendered to the Allies. People everywhere were confused about what it meant. Was the war over? Mussolini had been deposed and imprisoned by his government in July, an earlier moment of happiness but also uncertainty. This moment, September 8, 1943, might be another opportunity for celebration, or for more fear. The Allied bombings would certainly end with this armistice, they thought. But what about the German soldiers throughout Italy? Then, German tanks arriving in the towns made the situation clear: Italy was occupied, and its people were still at war.

The family was vacationing in a small village. Among the many prohibitions during the five years of the Racial Laws, from 1938 to 1943, Jews were forbidden from vacationing in certain places. Her family had managed to find places to go, and in the summer of 1943, they were in the mountains near Bologna.

"There were many Jewish people staying in this hotel, and the owner of the hotel was a great fascist; evidently he knew that the water was not so clear, and so he decided to have one foot on one side and one foot on the other."

After September 8, the family knew they would have to find a place where they were not known and could disappear, perhaps a big city. "To return to Padova was impossible because everybody knew us. We did not know where to go. We thought of Rome because we had friends there." But one night, her father heard two men talking in a hallway of the hotel.

"He heard one of them say that if he had to find a quiet place, he would go to Assisi. It was off the beaten path and there was a Fascist mayor, but he was an extremely good and humane man, the lawyer Fortini. Then my father, who was a very good Jew but who loved St. Francis very much, said, 'Okay, we will go to Assisi. That is how we made the decision, absolutely casually."

"My father was a mystic," she explained, "so he was always finding meaning. I saw on his night table from my birth, The Fioretti of St. Francis, and stories of the Hasidim, the Jewish mystics."

The decision made, the family managed to get a car to go to Assisi, which they said was their home. Of course, the countryside was alive with the movement of people, and so it was natural to see people escaping bombardments or returning to their homes. "The car broke down when we arrived at Pontassieve, a small city near Florence. Though small, the town was bombed often because there were many important train lines, and we found ourselves without a car in Pontassieve, finding it necessary to take a train full of refugees that was going south."

They got off the train in Arezzo and made arrangements for a car to leave two days later for Assisi. The night before their departure they heard the boots of German soldiers on the street below. "The soldiers were arriving because the German command had been bombed. Throughout the streets, they were searching for the person who was responsible for the bomb. We thought we would not be able to leave."

But the car did arrive the next morning, and after a few more difficulties, including another car breakdown, the family—Graziella, who was seventeen years old, her sister Miriam, who was ten, and her parents, Margarita and Emilio—walked up the last hill, to Assisi.

When Graziella and her family arrived, thousands of other refugees, mostly from bombed cities, were en route to Assisi as well—as many as seven thousand in all. The Viterbi family entered the town not expecting to know a soul, and they found a room in a hotel, Albergo Sole.

"We had our real [identity] papers. So, the hotel had to give the names to the police, and then the police in Assisi had to give them to the police of Padua. So, from Padua they sent some postmen to find us, and the owner, fortunately, he was an older man, a very simple man but clever, he understood the situation, and he said, 'They left for Rome just a few days ago,' and we were just a few meters from the place."

By chance, in the square, the Viterbis met a family they knew from Padua. They recommended that the Viterbis meet a certain priest who would help them, one Father Aldo Brunacci. Under the cloak of an effort to help the refugees fleeing the bombardments, led by Brunacci, an effort that grew to include Jews, the family name went from Viterbi to Vitelli. Two printers, father and son Luigi and Trento Brizzi, printed false identity documents for the family, as they did for the other Jewish refugees. They used family names from Southern Italy and made official looking stamps from towns under the Allied occupation in the south so that the Germans could not determine their validity. Graziella Viterbi became Graziella Vitelli. With their new names, the Vitellis moved into an apartment and lived openly, but hiding their identity.

"I had to write the story of our family and teach it to my sister every night, because for a girl of ten years, it's not easy to tell her, 'Now we are going by this name, remember your story.' She understood very well. But it was not easy." The family socialized little, so as not to accidentally give away their secret.

Seventeen-year-old Graziella ferried illegal documents herself, she said, bringing them from one place to another, hidden in her clothing. She felt happy to be tricking the German soldiers as she passed them in the street. Young people were often selected for this work, she told me, because the Germans were less suspicious of them.

I told Graziella about my earlier encounter with Father Aldo Brunacci, while visiting Gubbio, and asked her about his role in her experience.

"The underground movement was absolutely real, and the chief was the Bishop Niccolini, who was a marvelous man, absolutely. You know very simple like a fairy tale because he was confident. He was confident always in everything. He had all our real documents, because we had the false documents; all the real documents, he had, the bishop, and he put them behind the Madonna who was on the wall of his study, over his head.

"And so, the chief was the bishop, and there were two helpers, and one was Don Aldo Brunacci and one was Father Rufino Niccacci. So now Don Aldo says that Father Rufino did not do anything, but that is not true. I love Don Aldo Brunacci but have to say that really Padre Rufino Niccacci was very important too in this story. They were exactly, I think, approximately the same, but Don Aldo was more the intellectual, the mind, and Father Rufino was the other.

"He was always going here and there. I remember he had the sottana, the long skirt of the Franciscan brothers, and he was always like a wind. He was passing in the streets like a wind. Yes, he was really like this."

Graziella said she felt pride helping to deliver these false documents but had one experience of feeling alarmed. "One time, when I don't know why, they tried to find us. It was the spring of 1944. I was out with my sister, and we came back home, and we found a friend of the family, the Sicilian family, we met them in Assisi, who was waiting for us, and she told us, 'Come with me to my home because they tried to find you.'

So, we had to leave the house and go. And that moment, I was sure they had come for my parents because they were not there. They were already at this friend's home, but at that moment I was really afraid."

There was one other scare, and during another visit with Father Aldo Brunacci, two years later, I learned of that time, when the Viterbi family hid in his study. The priest was eventually arrested and imprisoned but released during the time of the liberation.

Like others everywhere, they all watched the movement of the Allies, as reported by whatever sources of information they had, including Radio London.

Graziella Viterbi. On the day of liberation in Assisi, Graziella stands in a doorway inside the apartment in which the family stayed during the occupation. Photo courtesy of Graziella Viterbi.

In Marina's living room that day, she and Graziella vividly recalled the moment it happened for them.

"We followed the troops [by radio] to Assisi, then we also began to hear the bombing. That last day before, or two days before, we saw the Germans were beginning to leave. And so, this was the sign that then it was not far," Graziella recalled. It was the British troops who arrived in Assisi.

"Here [in Rome] it was American," Marina said. She had managed to hide her identity as the nanny of a non-Jewish family, though for much of the time, her family hid in the countryside too, she told us. On the day the Allies arrived, Marina saw a man arriving on a tank. "My mother and I, we asked him where he was coming from. And he said 'Nebraska! I remember this name. Imagine the word!'"

Padua was further north and liberated ten months after Assisi. Meanwhile Graziella's family was deciding where to go next. In their absence, their house in Padua had been used by the Fascists, and afterwards a shoe manufacturer set up business there. Still, they did not know of this. Her father began to teach at the University of Perugia, near Assisi, and then found a job in Rome. Graziella began to study in Rome, and the family decided to move there, keeping their small apartment in Assisi.

Each summer, Graziella went to Assisi, and when she married and had children in Rome, the annual pilgrimage continued. When her husband died in 1992, Graziella moved back to Assisi, where she stayed until 1997, when the earthquake damaged her apartment. While the damage was being repaired, she moved back to Rome, where her children lived. Her Assisi apartment was the same one, from 1943, from Viterbi to Vitelli to Viterbi. From a teenage girl to an elder.

"I still visit my home in Padua every year, looking at it from the outside, of course." She never stopped closing her shutters as evening came. "My children always teased me about it." Father Brunacci and Graziella remained friends. "And he has a wonderful garden. I go very often during the summer, if I can bring my grandchildren, so we can go there, and they play. I am always waiting to go back to Assisi. But at a time, I will be too old to move again. If I wait a long time, I will have no more wish."

Sally and Marina joined in, urging Graziella to stay in Rome. "If you move back, you will not be near your grandchildren," Sally said. "You will regret it."

I later learned that Yad Vashem, the World Holocaust Remembrance Center in Jerusalem, honored Father Brunacci in 1977 as one of the Righteous Among Nations, the same year that they honored the Bishop, Monsignor Giuseppe Placido Nicolini, and the printers, Luigi and Trento Brizi. Father Rufino Niccacci had already been recognized, in 1974.

Orietta Vita Kohn

D URING THE EARLY YEARS, this project's momentum never flagged. It seemed to require little of me except to continue.

One day, a friend called a friend of hers in Sarasota, Florida. Frances Balter had Jewish Italian friends, older women like herself. She offered to set up appointments with them so we could meet.

A rainy January weekend in 2003, I stayed at a musty motel north of downtown Sarasota. The day was filled with three two-hour meetings. All three women were generous. Anna Maria Funaro's family had left at the start of the Racial Laws, as did Emma di Benedetto's family. Orietta's family remained.

Orietta and her friends all lived in a meandering development south of the downtown called Pelican Cove. A winding road passed similar-looking two-story condominiums, palm trees, and lush manicured bushes. The day I visited, the weather was cool and misty, and Orietta and her husband's apartment felt even more comfortable because of it. Mangroves rose from the bay to her deck, with its pots of red geraniums.

When I arrived, she led the way into the dining room, went into the kitchen, and returned with a small tin of miniature handmade biscotti, an espresso pot, and two porcelain demitasse cups and saucers.

"Tell me about yourself," she said, setting the table and the tone. Before I could interview her, she would interview me. So far, in three years, I told her, I had interviewed a priest who had been in Rome during the war, a woman whose Umbrian family scattered themselves in various hiding places in Rome during the German occupation, and another woman whose family hid in Assisi. I explained how I had met several times with a rabbi who ran a Holocaust education center. I started this project looking for the courage it might take to help someone in these circumstances, but I soon realized the courage it might take to try to survive. I relayed to Orietta how each person's story opened another window to understanding what happened in Italy. As I talked, I self-consciously stumbled over my thoughts.

"Okay, let me just ask you something," she said. "I don't want anything published with my name on it unless I have a chance to look at it. Okay?"

"Of course. Sure," I responded. "I intend to show people their transcripts."

"And a chance to correct any misquotes."

"And a chance to correct any misquotes," I echoed.

"It's very important," she said.

"And about my motivations," I said, picking up what I had been saying moments earlier, before I'd turned on the recorder, "I wish I could say clearly what they are."

"That's okay. That's all right," she said.

"I just know this is the first big project that I have ever felt compelled to investigate and understand."

"I want to be very honest with you," she said. "You will not get any dramatic story about I know so and so. I don't know so and so. And if I did, I have forgotten them. I am an old woman. Okay?" Even during this introduction, her lilting voice seemed to glide over her words. She poured coffee with the gentleness of a tea ceremony hostess, and then leaned into the conversation.

She said her friends, whom I had met that morning, had kept in close touch with people in Italy, but she had not. The only person in Italy she'd kept in touch with was her mother. "When I have gone back—many, many, many times—it was to visit my mother."

"All right," she said. "Now, I think you satisfied my curiosity, and you understand my prerequisites. Now, if I can help you, I'll be glad to."

She explained that her family members were "not at all observant." Her mother only went to synagogue each week because her father had been a prisoner of war in World War I, and her mother had promised God that if he returned, she would go to synagogue. She kept her promise, sometimes "dragging" Orietta along with her.

"When did things start to feel uncomfortable for your family?" I asked.

"I was in high school. It was a few weeks before school was to start. We were kicked out of school. A lot of people left, and a lot of people converted. And we could have converted. The laws said that if you converted before October 1, and if you were from a mixed marriage, you would be considered Aryan. Both of my mother's brothers and her sister converted, and their children; and we were under some pressure to convert also. My parents—I was seventeen, my brother was twenty-one—said, 'It's your life, your decision.' So we went into a huddle, my brother and I. When we told my father we would not convert, it was the only time I saw my father cry. He was relieved."

The Racial Laws forbade Jewish children from attending public schools. University students already enrolled could continue, but those not already admitted were barred. Orietta's brother had completed law school by this time, but Jewish professionals were severely limited in the practice of their work.

The laws were a shock to the assimilated Jewish population. But there were many years of "retrogression" before the Racial Laws, according to historian Michele Sarfatti. In his book *The Jews in Mussolini's Italy, From Equality to Persecution*, he talks about how warnings were sounded, sometimes rather loudly.

The Lateran Pacts of 1929 was one such warning. This was an arrangement between Mussolini and the church that resulted in the reinstitution of a state religion. The entire country was secular as a result of Italy's Risorgimento, and unification, in 1861, and completed in 1870, with the final battle of Rome, when the church lost its temporal power. But these Lateran Pacts gave societal standing to the church. Some in the Jewish community felt a sense of foreboding, says Sarfatti.

Because of the Racial Laws, Orietta's father found it difficult to make a living as an accountant. He closed his practice and moved to Milan, where "the right kind of person offered him a job as the financial advisor of their company."

The family eventually learned of a small chicken farm on Lake Maggiore, and a friend of her brother, whose last name was Boselli, offered to lend his name for the purchase of the farm.

Orietta found her own solution: "A cousin of mine who had connections in England thought the British Institute in Milan was independent and might be able to accept me. So, I went and saw Miss Isabel May, who was the director of the Milano branch. She stood in that room, pointing to the British flag there by the fireplace and she said, 'As long as that flag flies you can be here, and in fact, I will be your teacher.'"

Orietta earned her diploma in two years, and then went to help her brother on the farm. Eventually her family sold that farm, and her brother went to work on another farm. "You must have heard of Rizzoli Publishers. Mr. Rizzoli owned a little farm near Como, and my brother went to work for him at that farm." Soon, they were all living at the Rizzoli farm.

When Italy joined the war on the side of Germany, in 1940, and Allies began the bombardment of cities, industrial targets, and rail lines, exodus from the cities began. By the end of the war, half of Milan had been destroyed by bombs.

Mussolini's removal from power, in July of 1943, sent people to the streets. But what did it mean? What would happen with the war? The new leader, General Pietro Badoglio, quickly answered the question. He announced the war would continue.

Then, less than two months later, the secret deal between the Allies and Italy, the armistice, was announced, and again, people took to the streets. The war seemed to be over, again. But again, the people realized they were wrong when they saw German tanks beginning to appear in town squares. Indeed, the war was not over: instead the country was occupied, and the war on Italian soil had just begun. Jews had to hide, flee, or try to change identity, while the Allied troops fought the Germans. The race was on between the Allies moving up the peninsula and the German deportation machine.

"It was time to really hide, and through, I think, some people he had met on the farm, my brother made arrangements for us to live on the second floor of an inn, in a little town called Montorfano, near Como. And my brother, my father, and my mother never left the room. I did. I went to church every morning. I bought groceries. I had false papers by then. My name was Vittoria Bianchi. Four people living in a room. It was kind of a challenge, but we did it."

"Do you know where you got your false papers?" I asked.

"From Father Giovanni Barbareschi. I learned that after the war. Mrs. Barbareschi was my mother's corset maker, and she had this marvelous son that she was always talking about, who was a young priest, very good-looking, very charming. And I remember when we sold the farm, and I was unhappy about leaving my dog, Father Barbareschi said, 'I can use a dog.' I gave Gigi to him."

"Let's see, where were we?" she asked. I'd interrupted her memories.

"In that one room with your family," I replied.

"One day, returning from church, I heard the husband and wife arguing. Okay, it was very dangerous to hide us. We could have cost them their lives, and the woman was very unhappy about it. So, I went upstairs and said, 'It's time to go.'"

Orietta's family had one more option. They went to stay for a short time with a couple introduced by Mr. Rizzoli, Lina and Sandro Piazza, who earlier had offered to help. "They lived in a tiny little villa, in Milano, not in an apartment house. And they had limited means. For them it meant just adding more water to the soup."

Meanwhile, Father Barbareschi made arrangements for their escape to Switzerland. Milan was being bombed, and the trains were loaded with refugees, so it was easier for her family to get lost in the crowded trains leaving Milan.

Her family got off at a station near Varese, and there they waited for another group, which included relatives from Turin.

But that group was late, and the smugglers told Orietta's family they would have to wait another night before they could cross the border.

"'The Italian patrol that was going to let you through is no longer on duty,' they said, 'and you will have to spend the night here.' They had us climb one of those little ladders to the top of the hay loft, and they said, 'Spend the night here. Be quiet. We will be back tomorrow night at the same time.' And we were there about twenty hours. And of course, you never know because there have been cases where the smugglers got your money and turn you in because there was more money. You were at their mercy."

The guides did return the next night and led them to the border.

When they arrived at the crossing, Orietta continued, "The smuggler said, 'Throw your suitcases through the hole and pick them up in a hurry and run.' It was about three hundred yards. So, we did. We ran and we waited for the Swiss Patrol to come. And the Swiss Patrol came. They were very nice. I am sure you have heard that at that time a lot of people who had tried to get into Switzerland were sent back."

Of the twenty-eight thousand Jews accepted as refugees in Switzerland, about six thousand had entered from the Italian border. About the same number of Jews were turned back, according to Renata Broggini, in her book *Frontier of Hope*.

"And so, we had to wait for the police to get in touch with Bern [the capital], and it was not an easy wait. But we were accepted."

The family went to a gathering camp in the Italian part of Switzerland, where they were deloused and showered. Then they were sent to different camps. Her brother was on a farm in the German part of the country, and then was sent to a school for refugees, where he taught.

During this part of the story, Orietta began to cry: "Excuse me, I think I need a Kleenex. I still get emotional about it." In one camp, she remembered as Camp Herschberg, which she had health problems, including the cessation of her menstruation, which was common in these conditions of extreme stress.

She made requests to move, and for a time, her requests were ignored. She was frustrated and even frightened to feel unwell and away from her family. Finally, she was sent to her parents' camp in Lugano, where she stayed until the war's end.

When they returned to Italy, the family lived at the Rizzoli farm, using a little apartment there, because they did not have much money left. Orietta found a job as a secretary and then administrative assistant at the Milan office of the American Joint Distribution Committee, helping resettle refugees, who were coming from all over Europe.

While working there, she learned the National Council of Jewish Women in the US was looking for young women to come to the States to study social work on a scholarship, and then go back to Italy and continue to work with the Jewish Community. Someone told her she would be a perfect candidate.

"I said, 'Well, that sounds interesting. Let me talk to my family.' And I went home and told my family, and my poor mother said, 'Over my dead body,' and I said, 'You know what, I am going to go.' So, I came, feeling very guilty, but I did come."

Orietta studied at Western Reserve University, now Case Western, and met Howard Kohn, a young lawyer. After they married, she worked in various social service agencies, raised a family, and set up volunteer programs, helping elders get transportation, medical and psychological services. When the organizations were Jewish in nature, she worked for free.

"Did your experience during the war commit you to your Jewishness in any way?" I asked.

"Not out of suddenly becoming religious, but out of allegiance, loyalty, and memories," she said. "When I worked with the refugees, I heard quite a few stories. So, yes, I do. So do my kids, and my grandkids, though I never imposed anything on them. Not only in the Jewish sense, but in the political sense. You follow what goes on and you become very sensitized. You cannot say, 'It does not touch me, I don't care.' Yes, it does change your life."

Earlier I had told her that the president of the Union of Italian Jewish Communities (UCEI) in Rome said he thought all the witnesses had already been interviewed. But he still thought I should continue with my project. He said a new way of telling the stories might come, and one never knows where that might lead.

"As someone told you, I think all of the stories have been told. Are you doing something mostly for yourself? I wonder why. I don't want to destroy what you want to do. I'm just wondering."

I began to choke up. I was embarrassed. "I'm sorry. I don't mean to cry."

"Well then, now we can both do it. Would you like some Kleenex?"

"I guess it might be for me. I mean everything we do is ultimately for ourselves."

"Yes, that is true. Excuse me. I apologize. But do you have a sense of guilt because of your Italian background?"

My name signals that I am Italian American. In fact, my father's parents emigrated from Sicily long before the war, and my mother's family's background was a great mixture, mostly English. The culture in our household was not Italian, not the food, not the language. But I have an Italian background, and this project was connecting me to it.

"I always felt bad about that, I know I did. Who are these people that I have descended from?" I said. "So, yes, all my life I wondered, and I always felt a burden. And so, I am sure that is somewhere in my motivation."

"Okay," she said. "There were horrible people," she said. "But the people who hid us risked their lives. All in all, I found less prejudice then that what appears to be now. I think Hitler did not completely lose the war. But the young priest, the young lieutenant who didn't get paid, the people at the inn. So, when you feel funny about the Italians, some of them were animals, but the majority were helpful."

She was trying to comfort me, and I felt uneasy for having put her in that position. I tried to change course. "As you are talking," I said, "I also realize I wonder about myself. You know, there is the question."

"What would you do?"

"What would I do, underneath, I think, is the question. What would I have the courage to do? And if I were the one who had to hide, would I survive, would I mentally survive? I don't know," I said.

"You would mentally survive. You do. You become sensitized to many things. To this day, I get angry at things that other people don't notice. To this day, if I hear German spoken behind me. To this day, when I meet a German my age, I say, 'Where were you during the war?' We all have our prejudices, and I deal with mine."

"But also, that people have the strength to survive this sort of thing, and that people have the courage to help," I said.

"You have no choice; you would die. But the courage to help, that is what I wonder. Would I have had it? Would anybody else? That's why I think people who helped are so absolutely wonderful," she said.

"And they say it is not courage," I added. "You know, when you ask them, and they say, 'You just do what you have to do.' But some people don't."

"I remember when I thanked the family that took us in last. She was angry with me. She said, 'I did only what was natural. Quit thanking me.'"

"I really appreciate your conversation with me about your experience but also about my motivations. It is very important for me to know. At first, when you asked, I felt a little defensive and scared. I don't know what I thought—that you didn't trust me. But of course, why should you?"

"You came to me, you know."

"Out of the blue," I offered.

"Out of the blue, with my good friend Anna Maria, who just loves to take charge. She is a very dear friend of mine, as you know. But you know, what are you getting me into? But then I met you and I liked you, and so I am wondering, can I help you in any way?"

"You helped me a lot with this conversation."

"I hope you don't mind."

"You helped me a lot because you really touched something."

"I noticed. I noticed. I came out of my experience with a heightened sense of people being good. People being horrible too. That you cannot take away, when you hear certain things that happened. But when it comes to what happened in Italy, think of all the people that hid, were hidden. The emphasis is on the miserable, horrible things. And they happened, believe you me."

"Well, the temptation for the person who is not Jewish is to focus on the good. The focus on the good isn't right either. You have to tell the story."

"You have to tell the story," she said, "and you have to realize that this is the greatest thing about human beings: There is the good, and there is the bad, and there is the horrible. Can't help it. You cannot change it. So be it."

We made small talk for a time, about where I lived, in Great Barrington, Massachusetts. She knew someone who lived there. As I was packing up, she said, "I'd like to know what happens in your life and if you find yourself. I hope you don't mind. I become interested in people. I'd like to follow up."

A letter

That evening, I returned to my motel room with Chinese takeout and listened to the interviews. Again, I felt the power of the care given to me by the interviewee. I was the student. She was the teacher. I did not go into the project thinking of myself as a student, but as I thought about it much later, I realized that was exactly what I was.

Soon after the interview with Orietta, I sent her the transcript of our conversation for her review. In her return letter to me, postmarked from St. Louis, where she'd moved to be near her daughter and grandchildren, she included notes to the transcript.

When we met, she mentioned that before the war, her mother went to synagogue every week, as a promise to God when her husband returned from the first war. When she could no longer go to synagogue, she visited a little church, saying, "It is the same God." In one of the scribbled additions to the transcript, next to that part, she wrote that after the war her mother no longer continued this ritual. Perhaps she felt her earlier promise to go to synagogue for the safe return of her husband from the first World War had been in vain.

57

The House on the Square

LEARNING LEADS TO KNOWLEDGE of the immensity of all there is to learn. How could I organize what I was learning; how could I think about it? I decided to picture myself in a big palazzo of classical architecture situated on one side of a public square. Walking from room to room I looked out each window facing the square. From each room, I could see a part of the square and what was happening there; and after walking through the house, always looking out, I could put together a picture of what was happening outside. I knew that I would not connect all the stories and write a history. I would miss parts of the scene; I would certainly miss what had happened before and after, though I would learn what I could. Still, my responsibility was to pay attention to the pieces, to each view.

I have since learned about the use of an image of a house or other physical place, like a street with its shops, to store one's own memories for later retrieval. Cicero used this method of loci to prepare for his orations. He could go into his mind's map of shops along a street and retrieve the parts of his speech, assembling them as he "walked" along, going in and out of each shop. My house on the square had a different purpose but released me from tying up stories as complete packages, and instead allowed me to think of it more like an exhibit or a collage, rather than a work of history.

Virginia Gattegno and Lea Bellini

A taxi ride from Rome's Termini train station to the pensione between the Spanish Steps and the Tiber may deliver its passenger along a remnant of the Servian wall of the third century BCE, or Porta Pinciana, built six hundred years later. In June of 2004, the taxis passed hundreds of striped banners in rainbow colors, hung from windows as if heralding the soldiers' return from successful battle, or welcoming a cortege of foreign dignitaries. But these banners were printed with the word *pace*, for the marches against the war in Iraq: three million marched here a year earlier, the largest anti-war march in history. Though weather-worn, the flags seemed hopeful, even cheerful, the colors of assorted fruit-flavored candies in a glass dish. On a wall near the pensione, spray-painted in black: *Ne Islam Ne USA*. A few days later, on the train to Gubbio, a young man assured me that Americans would not reelect the president who had started this war.

A month to work in Italy was a luxury: Time off from my job, a sublease on my own apartment, and most of all the generosity of Giovanna Brunelli, who would be my host. She was the teacher in Gubbio who had become a friend beyond the Lenox Gubbio Exchange. Giovanna believed in my project, as vague as it was. The war was just a generation behind her, and she grew up living in its language and with its artifacts. A book that she kept included the story of her uncle, a priest, who had been active in the resistance during the German occupation. But my single mindedness—I was interested in stories of Jews— made an arbitrary wall between experiences of different people. Yes, the real wall, that label "Jew," had meant deportation and genocide. But after that month in Gubbio, and only years later, looking back in order to write, I saw that my wall had needed windows, for looking in and out, and doorways, for stepping into others' stories. When Italy was occupied, it was impossible for anyone to live a normal life.

Gubbio provided a welcoming base, but my primary mission for this month-long sojourn was to meet Virginia Gattegno Cipolato in Venice. Her cousin Amos Luzzatto had recommended that I meet her. Before coming to Italy, I wrote to her, and she responded. One morning, soon after arriving in Gubbio, I called to set up our appointment. She was not feeling well and asked me to call back the next day. The next day, she still was not feeling well. On the third day, she called and said to come for our meeting; she was feeling better.

That warm afternoon I took the train to Venice. A child kicked a ball outside the hotel, sending echoes across the stones. The air was mildly sea-damp, and the main streets at dusk were jammed with tourists. At a café, two young women scribbled postcards at the next table. Back at the hotel I prepared for the morning interview. After doing all the things to get ready—

check batteries, tapes, and microphone—I went to bed feeling prepared.

In the morning, I called to get directions to Virginia's home. She apologized: "I am sorry. I cannot meet you. I have lost my voice."

That day, walking along the big and little canals of Venice, I imagined her in many little scenes I saw: An old woman walking with a younger one, arms linked; an old woman walking alone. I found the Old Ghetto, and then wandered to the New Ghetto square. In the synagogue shop, I bought a book based on an interview with Amos Luzzatto, took it to the Gam Gam falafel restaurant and read. It was my first trip to Venice, but I was not interested in the canals or architecture, the shops or restaurants. Though I did not know where she lived, I wanted to stay as close to the experience of meeting Virginia Gattegno Cipolato as I could, though it seemed that I would go home without having met her.

Sitting on a stone bench looking at a synagogue shrouded in construction netting, the Nuovo Ghetto seemed a typical Venice neighborhood: tucked away, quiet. But it has its own history. The New Ghetto was created in 1516, on the site that was supposed to make way for the expansion of the copper foundry. Instead, the foundry, or ghetto, was not expanded, and apartment buildings were developed instead. Jews had been doing business and staying overnight but were not allowed to live in Venice until this seven-acre area of the Cannaregio district was planned to become the Jewish quarter. Christian occupants were evicted, and typically Venice, then a city state, an empire, decided where people it considered outsiders would live. This quarter, the New Ghetto, would have a locked gate at night. Later, the Ottoman Empire's Jewish subjects doing business and living in Venice would live in the slightly roomier

Old Ghetto, or foundry area, which was no longer functioning as such. The Jews living in the ghettoes came from various countries, with the later arrivals, the Levantine Jews, many of whom had moved to cities in the Ottoman Empire after their expulsion from Spain in 1492.

Like so much of Venice, this quarter was quiet, with no cars; the imagination can linger in antiquity. Then, two Holocaust memorials bring the visitor, fast forward, to the 1940s. In 1943, the chief of the Jewish community, Giuseppe Jona, committed suicide rather than hand over the lists of Jews to the Nazis.

Now, the presence of Italian Carabinieri, national law enforcement agency officers, guarding a synagogue and presiding over the square carries a modern visitor forward into the present, after the 1982 PLO terrorists killed worshippers in the main synagogue in Rome. Since that time, Italian national police have guarded Jewish sites.

"I will not meet Virginia, but still, I think of this trip as a pilgrimage," I wrote in my notebook. Traveling alone one hears stray conversations, like that of a young woman speaking of Jewish weddings and Protestant funerals as places where one sees lilies. There were graffiti: Venezia non Nazista; and I realized it might be time to change course and visit the archive in Milan, as Virginia's cousin also had recommended.

The next morning, on a train back to Gubbio, I ran into Jose Paul Koovanil, the seminarian who had interpreted the meeting in Rome in 2000, and another seminarian, both in black suits, when they boarded the train at a tiny station. We were both surprised to see each other in such an out of the way place, so far from Rome. Jose was living at a monastery in Umbria now. In the four years since meeting at Santa Croce Al Flaminio, Father Ribezzi's church, he and I had met a few times. Once he was the interpreter at another interview, with a nun in Rome, a Sister of Sion who remembered little from the war. We politely listened. After the meeting with her on a late afternoon in January, Jose and I had walked through the Vatican's Piazza San Pietro in the damp darkness where a creche was being disassembled. For a moment, I felt as though I were walking on a stage set after an important show, with a minor actor. He once told me that priests, when they perform the rite of the mass on the altar, in a large church where there are several priests, are performing the rite among themselves for God, and we in the pews are witnesses. That perspective on the ritual of the mass, which had previously felt rote and even mechanical in the pews, spread a fine aura of mystery around it. On the train that morning, during our surprise run-in, Jose said he remained in the period of consideration that seminarians go through before taking final vows. He was not sure of his future.

That evening back in Gubbio, Giovanna and I sat with her friend Alison until long after dark on the steps of a church in the Piazza Grande, then walked through the hilly streets, occasionally stopping to look at lit shop windows. Alison offered to arrange a meeting with her landlords, a couple who were children here during the war.

Gubbio, Lea Bellini

A few days later, Lea Bellini invited me to her apartment, and we sat at her kitchen table. Alison, the interpreter, sat next to her. Her husband, Gianni, sat off to the side, slightly away from the table. It was, it seemed, Lea who would tell the story.

To put Lea's story into context, Signora Ajo had said a German tank appeared in Gubbio on September 9, 1943. The announcement of the armistice the day before, the fleeing of the king and General Badoglio to the south, which was under the control of the Allies, and the German occupation—all within a couple of days—created complete chaos, in particular for the Italian soldiers, who were not given orders from the Italian Government, neither General Badoglio nor the King, before they fled. In the days after the armistice, many thousands of soldiers chose to leave the military, refusing to join the Germans or fight for the Repubblica Sociale Italiana. Instead, they shed their uniforms and either hid or joined the resistance.

Meanwhile, in Gubbio, too, of course, people waited for the movement of Allied troops up the peninsula. Allied bombardments continued; Germans occupied towns and cities. Italians were hostages to the privations of war, including hunger, and to the occupation.

On June 4, 1944, the Allies moving up the western side of the country liberated Rome. Moving up along the eastern half of the peninsula, Allied troops were moving toward Gubbio, and on June 20, 1944, troops arrived in Perugia to the south. On that day, June 20, 1944, partisans descended on the center to try to liberate Gubbio even before the Allies arrived, as had happened in other cities and towns. In Perugia, partisans worked to impede the fleeing Germans who were doing what they could do to block roads, eliminate bridges, and use any means to slow the movement of Allied troops in their pursuit. In a similar effort in Gubbio, one of the partisans killed a German officer and wounded a soldier. Though about to leave the area, the Germans were still in charge, and they reacted by rounding up forty Gubbio residents to be killed in reprisal. Forty men and women, having nothing to do with the murder of the officer but somehow identified, perhaps disliked, perhaps having anti-Fascist opinions, were arrested, brought to a school and imprisoned. Among them were a twenty-year-old mechanic, a thirty-nine-year-old orchestral musician, a thirty-nine-year-old bank employee, a sixty-one-year-old widow and mother of five sons, and Lea's father, Belluci Ubaldo, a mason. Lea, then a young girl, brought lunch to her arrested father, passing it to him through a window.

A group of the arrested were forced to dig their own mass grave. All the prisoners, including Lea's father, were then bound and gagged, lined up, and shot. Lea heard the shots.

Just days later, the Allies arrived. Liberation from German occupation and war brought people to the streets in celebration. This horrible period, as Signora Ajo had said, *un incubo*, a nightmare, was over. But in that celebratory day in Gubbio, a little girl named Lea was mourning the brutal murder of her father.

On June 22 each year, the city remembers the slaughter with an event held at the Mausoleum of the 40 Martyrs, a simple classical white limestone structure inside which forty marble sarcophagi with photos encircle the room. In 2004, the city marked sixty years since the murders. Hundreds of people, most of whom were not old enough to remember the massacre, came to recognize it.

Virginia Gattegno Cipolato

One afternoon, I arrived at Giovanna's to find a message: Virginia Gattegno Cipolato had called. She was feeling better, and she would see me.

With the sun rising I set out for Venice. This time, with her address in hand, I went directly from the train station to the vaporetto stop. The hold of the boat, where the passengers sat, was near water level, the engine burdened with the load. A half hour from the central station to the Lido, a sandbar in the lagoon, and a quick taxi ride brought me to an outer gate. Virginia buzzed me in, and I walked along a courtyard that led to her apartment.

While she made coffee in the kitchen, I sat in the living room, which was connected by a pass-through window. A window to a backyard was open, and a cat came in and went back out.

Virginia returned with espresso and biscuits and sat in a chair across from mine. She was tall, with white hair and serious lively dark eyes. She looked down as she thought, and spoke in a quiet, almost strained voice. Now, in 2004, perhaps the root problems that caused the Holocaust had not been solved, she said, and extremist and reactionary forces were making their presence known again. She wasn't sleeping well, and the state of the world felt heavy. Also considering a move closer to her daughters, she felt generally unsettled.

She liked to swim in the sea nearby. She had two daughters, Donatella and Raffaella, and her family, the Gattegno side and the Luzzatto side, were quite different, the first an artistic family and the other, a more intellectual group. She felt that she had inherited more of the Gattegno qualities.

One enters a relationship in an interview, and I felt then, with Virginia, as I often did, that I was the receiver, and she was the giver. But I did not realize the extent to which I was more than just a receiver. In my eight years as a journalist, I had learned to gather stories, but not to pay close attention to the effect the storytelling might be having on the teller. And listening, asking, clarifying—these actions are not passive. I usually focused on the topic I came to discuss, but the topic would stretch forward, into the person's present life. Occasionally, I would try to gently guide it back, but often I let it move where it went.

We talked for about an hour, and then she asked if, rather than discuss her experience of 1944, together we might watch an interview recorded years before by the Shoah Foundation Visual History Archive. And so, we moved to a small den, and she turned on the VCR.

A Shoah Foundation Visual History Archive representative had conducted the interview five years before. The interviewer had a soft voice, but she was businesslike, returning to the question she had asked whenever Virginia wandered beyond its scope.

Virginia was born in Rome. Her father had come from Salonika, a Greek city with many Jews, and a part of the

Ottoman Empire. When she was a child, the family moved to Anzio, in the south of Italy, and then in 1937, her father took a job as head of the Jewish school on the island of Rhodes. The family of five, with two daughters and a son, went to live on this little island in the Dodecanese chain off the coast of Turkey.

Life in Rhodes presented a rich stew of new ethnic tastes and styles for young Virginia, including Turkish, Spanish, and Greek, with an Italian overlay. She referred to the sensibilities that she encountered there as oriental. Many Jews had come to Rhodes, under Turkish control at the time, after being expelled from Spain and Portugal, in 1492 and 1493. Italy occupied Rhodes during the Italian Turkish War, and in 1923, the Treaty of Lausanne turned the island over to Italy.

Virginia's recorded story continued. The Gattegno family moved into "a delicious little house, very simple, very Mediterranean," with the terrace on top, and the kitchen across the courtyard. Virginia went to the Jewish school first, and then she moved to a public middle school. By now there was a fourth child, a baby boy, Giovanni. During the evening, in their living room, they played games, both musical and theatrical, and drawing games. The third child, Alberto, was the house philosopher. "He could have a conversation with the wall, he was so theatrical."

In a book she wrote many years later, *Per Chi Splende Questo Lume: La Mia Vita Oltre Auschwitz* (*This Light Shines for Whom: My Life Beyond Auschwitz*), Virginia said Rhodes was home to six synagogues. Living in Rhodes, she loved the sea, especially the beach. "Also, my sister Lea loved it: she always said the most beautiful moments of her life were there, at the beach."

In September of 1938, Italy's Racial Laws made her attendance at the public school illegal. The Jewish community scrambled to set up schools "in the biggest houses," she wrote.

She continued to study, and at an accelerated pace, and because she was still able to take the state maturity exams, despite the Racial Laws, she was qualified to become a teacher, and, she said, she taught at a Jewish school. At some point, her paternal grandmother, Sarah, came to live with the family. (In *The Jews of Rhodes*, Marc Angell talks about another school set up for Jewish students.)

War brought scarcity and hunger here to Rhodes, too. Some mornings, she went to school without having eaten. Her family squeezed a meal out of a couple of vegetables; often the black market was the only source of food and it, too, was often dry. She and her sister Lea worked, and, at some point, each one of them except the baby went to work to help the family. Still, she said, they did not feel their lives were in danger. The family was "an island, inside an island, inside an island": the family, the Jewish quarter—which she stressed to the interviewer, was not a ghetto—and Rhodes.

Virginia Gattegno Cipolato.
Photo credit: USC Shoah Foundation Visual History Archive.

German soldiers, not of the SS, occupied Rhodes in September of 1943, and she remembered them making their rounds in the quarter. On July 18, 1944, all the Jewish men on the island were summoned to appear at the German command headquarters, where their identity papers were taken from them. The next day, their entire families were summoned. The Turkish consul made sure the 42 Jews of Turkish nationality were spared deportation because of Turkey's neutrality, but the rest were held there for three days and then taken to boats for the first step in their long deportation from the Italian island possessions. In all, 1,822 Jews were taken from the islands of Rhodes and Kos.

Virginia remembers the last moments on Rhodes. As the Jewish prisoners filed to the boats, the German soldiers punched and kicked each of them. They beat each person as he or she walked past.

"I did not understand this," she said, stopping the tape. The two of us sat next to each other in the small room, she closer to the television. This action, remembered, could still activate the young woman's shock inside an old woman's body.

Thoughts, gathered back up and reassembled as a complete memory, re-membered to be told, are re-felt. When I sat with Virginia that day, all was so new to me: the Lido, Virginia, the open window, the cat coming and going. I may have been less sensitive than normal to the effect the experience of watching the interview might be having on her. Her cousin had warned me, if indirectly, by telling me about how difficult it was for her to talk to school groups about her experience. He had said that survivors spoke out of a sense of responsibility, despite the emotional repercussions of stirring up the old trauma. At one point, she told the interviewer that after a certain presentation in which she talked about her story, "mi sono crollata," like a building folds and falls under the impact of an explosion or seems to melt in a fire, when the walls and beams of the structure give out, *crollare*, collapse.

The interviewer asked how long the various legs of the trip took: first the boat, beginning on July 18, and finally the train, but Virginia did not give a clear answer. Unlike Primo Levi, whose memory seemed so intentional, to her, the memory of the trip was not one that she wanted to revive. She resisted attempts at precision, resisted dredging up detail. They did stop at Piraeus, she remembered, and at one point, they were loaded into trains. The Jews left Rhodes in mid-July, she said, and arrived at Auschwitz in August.

A few details from *The Jews of Rhodes: The History of a Sephardic Community:*

> On July 23, 1944, the Jews were crowded into three small freight ships. At the port of Leros, the ships from Rhodes met one from Cos [or Kos], which held one hundred Jewish victims from that island. After four days in Leros, they went to Samos, finally landing in Paraeus on July 31, 1944. Five Jews died due to the hardships of the voyage.
>
> Next, the prisoners were placed in a concentration camp near Athens. On August 3, they were crowded into trains and shipped to Auschwitz.

On that train, Virginia told the interviewer, they were given a taste of their new lives. There was no room to sit, nor was there a toilet. For food, there was a sack of raisins and a bag of onions, and she thought she remembered bread that her brother Alberto distributed.

"When we arrived at Auschwitz, a part of us was already dying. We had not eaten in days."

Upon the train's arrival at Auschwitz, SS guards screamed orders to separate family members, grabbing children from their mothers' arms. Virginia remembered mothers' screams. In her book, she writes of the formation of two lines, one for the very old and very young, and the other, of which she and her sister Lea were a part. This was the last time she saw her mother, grandmother, and baby brother.

In her interview, she stressed the sense of grayness. Mud, dark barracks, cold. "There are no colors at Auschwitz."

"They undressed us completely, men and women. They shaved us completely from head to toe…from the first moment, the destruction of the person."

"We had to learn five orders [in German] for survival," she said, and that memorizing began the moment they were assembled to be deported. First, of course, they had to figure out what the words meant.

"Our reaction was one of disbelief, absolute inability to react."

The young and old were immediately brought to gas chambers and killed. Her baby brother and her grandmother were among them.

The interviewer asked her to say her tattooed number. She pulled up her sleeve to show the inside of her arm, and without looking, said A24324. She never looks at it or thinks about it, she said.

From the warm island of Rhodes to the fall and winter of Poland, frozen feet. At one point, they were issued wooden clogs, frozen feet inside wooden clogs. Orders, in German, and then the cacophony of the prisoners' languages. One prisoner, learning that she was Italian, called her a Fascist.

Inside the barracks, prisoners slept on bare wood. Latrines were outdoors. Mornings, still dark, the bell would ring for the prisoners to go outside. This ritual continued through fall and into winter.

Virginia worked moving stones from one place to another, and then she was transferred to another building, where she braided rubber and leather-like materials. She never understood the purpose of her work: "It seemed stupid."

She remembered the cold more than the hunger, though watery soup and a piece of bread could not sustain them for long.

Every few minutes, Virginia would direct the interview to the end of her time at Auschwitz, as if talking about the end would end it. She accomplished this, arriving at the end of Auschwitz by summarizing the experience and even by talking about her wishes for the end while there. "If there is a prayer, it is the only prayer I said. 'I want to live just one hour after Auschwitz.'"

In January of 1945, Germans began to leave Auschwitz in advance of the coming Russian Army, forcing fifty-eight thousand prisoners on death marches; and the day before the Russians arrived, they blew up the last operational crematorium. Virginia and her sister happened to be in the infirmary when they left.

She stopped the tape once to tell me about a hero, a fellow prisoner, whom she met after the Germans left, before the Russians arrived with food. Her sister was weaker, and so Virginia went foraging for something to eat in the camp. She found a frozen turnip and tried to find some way to eat it. She found a can of tomatoes and could not open it.

Then she found a woman making some type of cakes with flour and water. The two women did not speak the same language, but they communicated, and the woman told Virginia that if she could chop wood for the fire, she could have one of the cakes. Virginia raised the ax to strike the wood, and fell. She did not have the strength to lift the ax. But the woman gave her a cake anyway, which she brought back to share with her sister. They would survive another day. About the woman giving her the cake, she said, "This is heroism."

But to expect this type of behavior of people in these conditions *non e giusto*, is not right, she said. To maintain any dignity, to not steal from other prisoners, this goal was nearly impossible. Never mind heroism.

The first meal was a substantial soup, apples, and something Virginia called cereal. Luckily her digestive system could handle it. Some could not keep the food down. People continued to die, she said. They had already reached the point of no return. Virginia was assigned to work in the kitchen.

The war continued, and Russians were responsible for the camp for about six months. After the bombing of Nagasaki—this is the marker she used to mark the end of the war—a group of Italians set out for Italy, not knowing which trains to take or where to change trains. The family's survivors, Virginia and Lea, set out for Rome, where they had relatives. She learned that her brother Alberto had died shortly before liberation. She told me about a Sicilian man, Salvatore, who accompanied them on the train all the way to Rome, jumping off when the train stopped to get them food from fields. They never knew how long a train might stop—a couple of minutes or hours—and never knew if Salvatore would make it back in time. He always did.

When they arrived in Rome, they spent time in a hospital and then a pensione run by the Sisters of Sion. A friend from Rhodes came to visit her in Rome and suggested Venice as a place for Virginia to live.

Near the end of the interview, she said something to the interviewer that struck me: "I am not a great person, but I can say one thing for myself: Auschwitz did not destroy me."

When the tape was finished, she led me back toward the living room. It was time for her to rest, she said. I didn't know what to offer to her. Should I bring her something to eat? I knew I should give her something, but it seemed that she was tired and ready for me to leave. She said that it was time to light a candle for Shabbat. Would I like to light it with her? We returned to the pass-through window ledge between the kitchen and the living room. It seemed days had passed since she made our coffee. She lit one candle. Then she gently hugged me and wished me a good Shabbat.

The memory of leaving is always less acute, less clear. Getting back to Venice the same way I came—by taxi and then vaporetto—is completely hidden by the awe that I carried with me that night. People have survived hell and returned to life and carried on, as mothers and fathers, as teachers, lovers of dance and art, like Virginia, wounded but carrying on. That deep wound of the world, the Holocaust, or Shoah, the disaster, living in bodies that remember, giving the story to others so that they will carry it too, in their small way. Later, I would go to Yale and then Columbia University, where the Shoah Visual History Archives were available for viewing at various times, and record, and then listen to Virginia again and again.

Her story and her entrusting of it to me, the giving of her physical presence that day, and then including me in her simple Shabbat ritual before saying goodbye. All her generosities were lodged inside me. I learned certainly, but not only that. I was somehow changed. I began to light the Shabbat candles every Friday, and have done so since that early Friday evening in June of 2004.

Rome, June 2004

I T WAS TIME TO LEAVE ITALY and go home to my job. Leaving meant a last visit to Rome, to a city that was becoming more familiar. This time, I attended a huge international oral history conference in one of the buildings on the Campidoglio, designed by Michelangelo, with its broad staircase, the cordonata, leading to a geometric black-and-white square. Inside the city hall there, speakers gave opening remarks, and the hundreds of participants moved outside to have cocktails overlooking the Roman Forum.

A conference host, Alessandro Portelli, had written a book about a Nazi massacre of 335 Italians in the Ardeatine Caves of Rome. In the book, he demonstrated how memory is often shaped by the opinions held at the time of the event—in the case of memory of the Ardeatine massacre, the political beliefs, right and left, in particular. Those on the right believed those on the left were responsible for the Nazi massacre—they could have turned themselves in, they reasoned, for killing the soldiers. But Portelli demonstrated that the Germans gave no time for turning oneself in. By the time people knew about the massacre, it had already had happened. *The Order Has Been Carried Out* is the name of the book. With fixed left and right identities as were common in Italy at that time (and as I began to notice in my own country—fixed political identities, with fewer middle or true independents), the memory of what happened was directly related to one's political affiliation at the time of the event.

The conference was filled with people confidently talking about their work over cocktails, looking at the Forum's ruins as the sun's rays slanted across the landscape below us. How would I talk about a project that had begun as part of a reporter's ordinary day and was changing to something else, perhaps it was oral history, about whose form and shape I knew so little. As usual, at events like this, I listened. Their work was a profession; this meeting was a way to meet others doing related work. It seemed a mistake to have signed up, but it was instead the beginning of a new way to look at the stories I was hearing.

Finally, about to go home, a last meeting. Having received the Olivetti grant in 2001, to interview Signora Ajo with students, I had become interested in the family of the Olivetti company, in part to understand the reason I received the grant. Laura Olivetti invited me to meet with her. She was the granddaughter of the founder, Camillo, who was intensely curious, an industrialist socialist, born a Jew, and she was the daughter of Adriano, anti-Fascist and later, a well-known industrialist and a senator. On my way to meet her, in the taxi, I heard Louis Armstrong's voice singing "What a Wonderful World," the same song I had heard while on hold waiting to make the appointment with her a few weeks back. These little coincidences lifted simple moments—like this taxi ride—to something else that I could not put my finger on, but they made me feel happy, like I might be in the right place. After our meeting, she offered access to the company archives in Ivrea, in the north, and loaded me with books: another blessing.

It is impossible to avoid a conversation about political right and left.

Rather early on, one of the books I found in English was Alexander Stille's *Benevolence and Betrayal, Five Italian Jewish Families Under Fascism*. In fact, for a time, it was my guide. The first family Stille features in the book is headed by the father, an Italian Jewish Fascist.

When this man returned home from the First World war, he found, "Millions of people mourning their dead." Economic crisis led to riots, looted food shops. Peasants and workers, trade unionists and others, disrupted everyday life to call attention to their hardships. Many looked to the Russian revolution for inspiration.

Stille says the left terrified the middle classes, going "out of its way to alienate the millions of soldiers returning from the front." Having been against the war effort, socialists prevented war veterans from joining their party. And some engaged in even more dramatic actions against returning soldiers.

At the time Mussolini's group of Fascists first met in Milan, in 1919, the atmosphere was one of unease, disruption. Fascism was a thuggish response to conditions, but it is easy to underestimate the power of a promise of order, even brutish order. When the Blackshirts took their trains to Rome, in 1922, and the king invited Mussolini to form a government, rather than listen to the pleading of his prime minister, who asked him to repel the insurrection with his army, his decision was misguided and cowardly, but perhaps not surprising.

When I met Stille much later, he said he thought it was important to start with this particular man. I said I understood. We assume we know who the Fascists were, but we do not necessarily know. In Italy, Jews were also Fascists, in approximate proportion to their numbers.

Historian Michele Sarfatti explains this may be because Jews tended to be patriotic and politically active, and they were represented all along the political continuum, perhaps even more so on the left than the right. Fascism was seen as a possible solution to chaos by many, and then others held a wait-and-see attitude.

Now we can read what happened and try to understand. And we can try not to do the same thing again. We can recognize our own role in stopping or abetting tyranny, or at least try to understand dynamics at play in our own countries.

Liliana Picciotto

IT WAS TIME to visit the main archive on contemporary Italian Jewish history in Milan.

When I arrived in Milan, the cab driver at the train station had to look at a map to find the block-long quiet residential street where CDEC, the Contemporary Jewish Documentation Center, was housed. Across the narrow street from the four-story building with the wrought iron locked gate, the national police sat in their car. The building belongs to the Jewish community of Milan, and as mentioned earlier, the national police have guarded Jewish sites since the 1982 Palestinian terrorist attack at the Great Synagogue in Rome. A simple, small building and archive in a residential neighborhood was no exception.

CDEC's front hallway, with bulletin boards and tacked announcements, led straight to a stairway. Librarian Marina Marmiroli had answered my e-mail inquiry, and it was she who came down a few steps, cheerfully signaling me to come upstairs.

"Why would you want to write another book?" she asked, sweeping her arms toward the stacks of her domain. "There are already so many books." I liked her right away. She had an air of collegial competence, dark coiffed chestnut hair, and an overall fine and warm finish. She invited me to sit and wait at the end of a long table in the library's reading room while she went to find Liliana Picciotto.

An archive, with its mysterious and private codes of access, and a person, with his quirks and habits, require distinct, individual, approaches. Some of us are more inclined to trust our abilities with people, feel more comfortable talking and listening. Others prefer to go into the inner rooms where they may find something few have ever seen and begin an unraveling pursuit of excited discovery. I have little trouble asking people to tell their stories, but codes of access to inner rooms, in another language, can intimidate. If I persist, it is worth the effort.

Liliana Picciotto appeared by the table where I was reading, introduced herself, and asked right away if I had read Alexander Stille's *Benevolence and Betrayal*. I told her that I had, but I wanted to write individuals' stories using their own words and hoped to do some research here, spend some time in the archive. Who had I interviewed, she asked. When I mentioned Graziella Viterbi and Virginia Gattegno Cipolato, she seemed to let go of some reluctance. She knew these women. She did not know Maria Perla Ajo from Gubbio, or the people who had moved to America and whom I had interviewed there, but it seemed that I had passed one test.

Liliana is a star in this world. If there are a few well-known experts on the Holocaust in each country, she is in that group, at the head of it in Italy. She and her colleague Michele Sarfatti have written many books, two of which I saw in Rome on the first visit, at the Union of Italian Jewish Communities library, and one is foundational: *The Book of Memory*. Inches thick, it includes the names, destinations, and fates of each Jew deported from Italy during 1943 and 1944. This archive in Milan, CDEC, where she had worked for her entire adult life, holds primary records, and Liliana knows every piece of paper in it.

Cocooned inside layers of hallway and office, hundreds of stacked boxes on shelves hold memories of Italian Jews, most dealing with the period of 1938–1945: letters, journals, postcards, and diaries. Government documents and newspaper articles from the same period recreate the setting for the individual stories. Thousands of pieces of paper represent the will to carry memory into the future. Memory's hope is with these pieces of paper—the official and the personal—in the archive. Liliana and a small cohort of colleagues are its keepers.

A researcher could come here and open one archival box and spend hours in 1938 or 1943, with one family or one story. That is what I did that afternoon, beginning with a file on Fausto Levi, from Milan. Inside there was a postcard, the front of which was printed, Vinceremo! We will win!—a motto of Mussolini. On the back was the date, December 7, 1943, along with the words of Fausto, written in code, to his wife. *We are going to visit Mrs. Poland*, he writes, telling her who is with him: his cousins from Genoa and his aunt and uncle from Rome. *I hope you did not bring the suitcase on Friday because it would have been lost like all the other packages. Please stay calm and prepare for anything. My last thoughts will be for your mother and for you, my beloved.* It was addressed to Via Proccacini, just a few blocks away from CDEC. I wrote down his words in my notebook. I read other files, but I walked out with the vivid image of that postcard, its *Vinceremo!* on one side and words of Fausto Levi in transit to Poland on the other.

During that first visit, Liliana and Marina told me that I would be welcome to come back. CDEC director Michele Sarfatti gave me an interview about his work, and we talked about my project. It was time to apply for a fellowship, to find a way to come back to Milan for more than a week or two. As I walked down the stairs to the first floor and buzzed the door to get out, a man holding a tray of espressos, the scent of warm coffee following him, ran down in front of me and held the door.

⁕

During my second brief visit to CDEC, in November of 2005, I tried to unravel the reasoning of the archive's system. Liliana pointed out a looseleaf binder in the corner, but instead I pulled the boxes down according to their position on the shelf. I started by looking at files with family names.

The Boehm file: Margherita Luzzato Boehm and Michelangelo Boehm and their children: letters, and some government documents. A puzzle without all the pieces. It seemed that some family members survived by escaping to Switzerland, but a father and mother were killed in Auschwitz. After the war, someone whose name did not match the rest of the family dutifully documented his search, to various officials and agencies, to learn of family members' final fates. I spent an hour with the file and found that little by little the power of the accumulated parts seeped into my consciousness. Before I could realize it, I was struck by its impact. I knew I would have to return to this file when I had more time, and I vowed to find a way to come back.

Touching the paper, seeing handwriting or even the typeface of a manual typewriter—on a letter, a journal, a postcard—

brough me closer to the person writing it than would reading a computer screen or even a book. I knew the time of touching paper in boxes would end, but that was the organization of CDEC when I was there, and though it was set up in what seemed an inscrutable way, as I untied the boxes' ribbons and pulled the documents out, I felt as though I might be listening to the people themselves.

Liliana suggested that I watch her documentary film *Memoria.* I put on earphones in one corner of the videoteca, a bright long room with windows outside the cocoon of the archive, and watched. There was a camera and an interview taking place on the other side of a stack from me. But soon I was at full attention to the small television screen. The film started with an old man singing a popular 1940s song, *"Mamma son Tanto Felice"* ("Mama, I Am So Happy"), and it quickly pulled me into its sadness.

Faces of old men and women close to the camera. Someone talks about being kicked out of school because of the Racial Laws. One elderly man remembers the end of childhood, early morning, October 16, 1943, when he and his family were pulled from their apartment in Rome and a few days later sent to Auschwitz. Another man, from Florence, begins to cry when he remembers the Jewish children killed in the concentration camps.

In the film, I saw Liliana from the back. She was walking with an old woman through the San Vittore prison in Milan. The old woman was telling Liliana about how, as a young girl, she and her father were held in that prison before being taken to the Milan train station and deported to Auschwitz. Together the two women walked slowly away from the camera as we watched, hearing their shoes on the cement. I saw Liliana skirt the camera's viewfinder, leaving in full frame the older woman walking away. (This survivor, Liliana Segre, would later become Senator for Life, as recognition of her work in Holocaust education.)

After watching the film, I walked to Parco Sempione, five minutes away, and there, sitting on a bench watching the passing of an ordinary day in Milan, my mind brought me to 1938, the Racial Laws, as people crossed the paths in front of me. They were headed to lunch or to their homes, and I saw them doing the same thing in 1938 and then 1943. That day, in the park, I decided to invite Liliana to come to my hometown in Massachusetts to show her film. I raised money, organized three screenings, and, in the fall of 2006, squired Liliana and her companion, Aurelio Ascoli, around for her to give talks in three cities in Massachusetts.

The summer before they arrived, I received word from the Fulbright Commission that my project had been approved and that I would receive a fellowship to live and do research in Italy.

One day, driving with Liliana and Aurelio for her presentation to graduate students at Clark University in Worcester, we discussed my upcoming move to Milan. That day, Aurelio volunteered to help me in my search for apartments. I had already found two, one while chatting at a Centro Primo Levi reception for Rome's mayor, Walter Veltroni, in New York. I found the other apartment online. Back in Milan, Aurelio looked at the two places and recommended the one I had found by word of mouth in New York. The other one, he said, was amateur.

In late January of 2007, I arrived in Milan, and went directly to the apartment that Aurelio had recommended. For nearly five months, I would have a luxury that I had never had: to work on this project, without worry about making a living; to pick up all the pieces I had gathered one at a time over seven years; and finally, to have time to contemplate how it all fit together, in Italy, the place where it had happened.

Part Two:
In the Place of Memory

Milan, January 2007

Arco della Pace, at one end of Parco Sempione, Milan.
(Judith Monachina)

A CONSTRUCTION FENCE surrounding Napoleon's arch was covered in graffiti. The arch and the graffiti presided over a circular piazza. A man wearing a black duck cloth jacket crossed on a bicycle. Other people walked their own diameters, entering here and there, passing straight from one side to the other. Just beyond the piazza, inside Parco Sempione, a hardy green covered the ground around a pond and between the paths and tall pines. The Sunday afternoon was warm enough for people to sit on benches and most of them were taken.

"É libera?" I asked an old man if the space on his bench was free. Yes, he gestured with his eyes to the empty half. I sat and watched people walking on the wide gravel path, and looked for clues of life in their clothing, stray words, gestures. Small groups, mothers and fathers with strollers, young ones and old ones apart or together. I held myself close and watched, but I liked talking with old people.

"It is warm for January," I said; he agreed. "Do you live in Milan?" Yes, he said, but he was originally from Potenza, in the south. He came here to work many years ago, too many to remember, and though he had always wanted to go home, he never did, and did not want to go anymore.

"People there work with their hands," he said, looking at me, as if I would naturally agree that it was a flawed way of life. His eyes were clear blue. I knew nothing of his story, and he did not explain.

His tweed jacket seemed a part of him. On his lap lay a brochure that said Scientology on the outer flap. He looked down as much as out. Then he decided to tell me something. One year, soon after he arrived in Milan, it rained and rained and rained, for the entire year. The trees died. The plants—that was the word he used—all the plants died. "From that time on, it never rained here. Year after year, no rain."

Then we were quiet, just watching people. The story he told was not an accounting of historical events, but something between that and a metaphor. A deep unknowing pervaded my being in this new place, and so his story, whose meaning I could not know, fit with my general sensation. He expressed what he felt, and though I could not truly understand, I could imagine the feeling when he expressed it as a year of rain.

As a stranger, a foreigner cannot know the inside of a culture or a language without years of immersion. The challenge began here, with this story of rain. After a few more words, I said goodbye and walked back through the park toward Napoleon's arch and home.

There, street names told another kind of story, the official memory. Via Piero Della Francesca, named for the painter, leads to Via Angelo Poliziano, named for the Renaissance poet and philosopher. Piazza Gramsci, named for the political philosopher, writer, and communist politician, who was imprisoned by the Fascists in 1926 and died in 1937, is a square surrounded by outdoor restaurant seating, a play park for children, and a place to cross through on foot from one neighborhood to another.

On the second floor of a modern building on Via Poliziano, my apartment had pink travertine floors. A glass door to the balcony looked out to the cortile and beyond, to a tall reddish-brown building with most of its modern mechanical white shutters half closed. The whole building seemed to be winking; at night the building's shutters closed, and it seemed to disappear.

I unpacked. The travelling shabbat candlesticks I had given my fiancé in our first year, and the small sand-colored notebook, though I had not opened it since the first meeting with Father Ribezzi.

Soon, I was alone. My fiancé, who came with me to help with settling in, had left. He bought me a tram map; we had dinners together, explored neighborhoods. I accompanied him to Linate airport and then sat for hours in Parco Sempione. I watched women caregivers from Ukraine and other eastern European places enjoying a day off together.

Inside a nearby church, an old woman quietly cried. I lit a candle for her.

Shortly after my arrival, news outlets announced that twenty-six Americans were indicted by the Italian government for a 2003 CIA kidnapping of a suspected terrorist on a street in Milan. It was part of the American practice at that time of Extraordinary Rendition, the removal of suspects to so-called dark places, where they were interrogated and tortured. The image of the US abroad was frayed by its response to the terrorist attacks of September 11, 2001, in particular the Iraq war, and this practice did not help with its image. I was concerned by the warnings posted on the American Embassy site in Italy, telling Americans to avoid big crowds, to avoid demonstrations. I was an American, learning about a period in which a different history had unfolded, Americans fighting the Germans and Fascists. But the modern America was the one that accompanied me along the streets. It accompanied me whether I entered a kebab takeout or walked into a pastry shop.

At my apartment, organizing my materials, notebooks, computer, I pulled out the sand-colored notebook. I feared there might be nothing in there, not an interview that had sparked a change in my life's course. And even if it were full, what would I do next?

Aurelio Ascoli

Aurelio and Liliana gave me an evening tour around the historic center, which was anchored by the medieval Sforza castle, with its graze-lit battlements and towers. Turning the car outside the church refectory that holds the Last Supper, Santa Maria Delle Grazie, Aurelio nodded toward the ubiquitous graffiti on the building facing the church. "Why does Milan not do something about it!" he stormed as he pulled the wheel. Not far away, he pointed out the building where his father had worked, Edison Company of Italy; a lipstick red sculpture dominated a nearby piazza.

Within days, Napoleon's arch, the Sforza castle, with its two arms reaching an eighth of a mile in either direction, and a huge Armani billboard bearing a blond model in a short red dress, leaping in midair as if cheering for a football team, became visual anchors, around which the orange trams hummed.

My apartment was just a fifteen-minute walk to Via Eupili. Two floors up, in the archive, I lifted the shutter to the window over a single school desk, turned to the stacks to select a box, and brought it back to open it. Sorting through the boxes of letters and articles was something like exploring the streets: which ones would I come back to; which ones would I see only once.

Very soon, I understood the vastness of what I must learn. I read in the archive, in a language that I still translated deliberately, not fluidly. I also wanted to simply be in the place where it had happened and encounter the part of the history that lives inside people, in their ideas. While the hundreds of files promised to teach, while I could, I wanted to hear the stories of people who were sitting in the room with me or driving the car. So I tried to do both: read the documents, and listen to people like Aurelio Ascoli.

The number 27 tram to Aurelio's home passes the vast Palazzo Giustizia court complex and the Largo Marinai d'Italia. The city lost half of its buildings in the Allied bombardments of 1942 and 1943, and looking closely, one could see evidence of the destruction: the pre- and postwar butt up against each other. Many of the buildings stretching along Viale Piceno have sharp modern edges and balconies set into them rather than jutting out from the facade. It was a comfortable street: the people seemed to live well, to have enough, certainly more than enough cars: many small ones were nose in on the treed median, making it a parking lot.

Several floors up, in his kitchen, Aurelio made a "tall" espresso and set up on the stove what he would later make for dinner. He insisted on catering to my American-ness, with tall cups and promises of an early dinner, and he did not listen to my genuine protests.

The living room was half of a very large, light area, with long windows leading to a balcony and the street. In the other half, the ample dining furniture gave the sense of family life lived, well-used fabrics, the warmth of wear. The nine-story building was constructed in 1964, he told me, on the rubble of war, on what had been a street of two-story buildings. As an engineer and professor in his younger days, it was to this apartment that he came at the end of the day. Still, alpine ski trips with grandchildren continued; he rode his bicycle to do neighborhood errands. He plucked memories whole from the past.

In 1990, he said, in front of two-hundred people who were assembled at the Societá del Giardino in Milan, then sixty years old, he stood up in the audience to address the special guest, Prince Amedeo of Savoia, duca di Aosta, third cousin of King Vittorio Emanuele III. For fifty-two years, Aurelio had wanted to say these words about the Racial Laws of 1938 to someone close to the king, and now he had his chance.

"When the law came out," he said to the prince, "I felt insulted not as a Jew but as an Italian. For me King Victor Emanuele III ceased to be the king of Italy, not when he abdicated, but when he put his signature under that law."

Everybody started to applaud. "You would think the walls might come down," Aurelio told me, "with the applause that I had."

Inside that older man addressing the prince was the eight-year-old boy who remembered a certain day in September, 1938. The air was warm; school would start soon. His family sat in the parlor and listened to a radio address.

"I remember hearing it on the radio. I said to myself, what is this king that puts his signature on the law. So I decided that was not my king anymore." The monarchy, often remembered fondly for its role in the beginning of the Italian republic, became moot, or worse, for young Aurelio when the king signed the Racial Laws.

Remember that earlier, in 1922, the king had withheld his signature on the decree requested by then Prime Minister Luigi Facta to stop the Blackshirt Fascists, who were boarding trains toward Rome. Feeling safer with the Fascists than the Socialists, the king made many decisions, including putting his signature to the many updates—tightening the screws—of the Racial Laws.

During this time, Aurelio's father, an engineer who designed high voltage lines, rose in the ranks of the Edison Company of Italy, and was promoted to a managerial job in nearby Monza, where Aurelio was born. The couple had three children. He said he was the "chevalier fra due dame," but then he laughed and gave me another image: "a salami sandwich, and I was the salami."

As a young man, Aurelio's father also achieved a status in the Masons that Aurelio remained proud of. But Masonry was outlawed by Mussolini, and Aurelio remembered a scene. "There was a double flight of stairs to go to the cellar, and the central boiler was in the mezzanine of the stairs. I remember it was painted silver. I remember one Sunday morning, my father was home; he was wearing his home jacket with a pipe in the pocket, and I saw the Masonry symbols, the apron, the gloves, the hammer, the compass, the set square—throwing them into the fire. My mother assisted my father. I remember asking, 'Why does daddy burn all these things?' 'You cannot understand now, but when you are grown up you will understand,' she said."

In 1935, the family moved back to Milan. The dictatorship had a decade to establish deeper roots by the time they promulgated the Racial Laws in September of 1938, an early piece of legislation tht singled out the lives and livelihoods of Jews. The right of children to attend public school was taken away. By the end of 1938, Jews had lost their right to own businesses employing one hundred or more people; their right to serve in the military; to employ "Aryan" household help; and they were required to declare their assets. The list of prohibitions is dizzying. Jews could no longer listen to the news on their parlor radios as Aurelio's family had done: Radios were forbidden.

Centuries of church teachings against Jews had established one anchor in the foundation of these Racial Laws.

A year before the Racial Laws that excluded him from school, something happened to Aurelio that Sarfatti might include in what he called "retrogression," which included incremental rather than sudden change, like the earlier sting felt by some Jewish leaders with the Lateran Pacts. Aurelio's own experience happened much later, one year before these Racial Laws, though a boy of seven years would hardly have seen it as such.

"Of course, until the third [grade], I had a lady teacher, because it was considered lower elementary school; and the fourth [grade], I had a man teacher. And there the first difficulties started, because I wouldn't say he was a Fascist—he was a devoted Catholic—but he was impregnated with fascist propaganda. So, it started to feel that I was different. There was no straightforward persecution, but you could feel a thick air.

"The Fascist regime established a competitive essay to produce a nice composition about our duce and our king. And here comes this Fascist officer with his uniform, with leather boots, and he calls all the children by alphabet. And since I was the smallest one, I was in the first row, and since my family name starts with A, I was first or second or third. I raise my hand, I say, 'Sir.' He says, you be quiet. When he finishes the roll call by Z, I remember there was a Z named boy—Quinzio Zabban—he said, 'So you Ascoli, you sit down in the last row.' And so, I started to cry. I said, I am the smallest one, so if you send me to the last row, I can't see anything. He said, 'but that's the rule, you go to the last row.' So, I cried.

"I remember, I wrote the composition with falling tears. It was my first experience, and of course, I failed that essay. I failed it."

One year later, Aurelio was transferred to another public school. In municipalities with a certain number of elementary school students, schools were obligated to set up separate sections for Jewish children. Sarfatti explained, "The government gave these concessions, not wishing to see the principle of compulsory education impaired." Another decree allowed Jewish organizations to set up schools, and for Jewish children to take the state exams. Jewish university students could continue studying until they graduated, but no new Jewish students would be admitted to the universities.

Aurelio's sister Mirella, sixteen years old, was expelled from public school. The Jewish community organized a school in Via Eupili, in two buildings, one of which is now the CDEC archive, he told me. "Those two small houses were the seat of the high school, which, in fact, I attended the next year."

That was how I learned that CDEC had been the Jewish school during the Racial Law period. Perhaps there was a plaque, but I had not seen one. The children would have come from throughout the city, many approaching that neighborhood for the first time. Using Napoleon's arch as their landmark, they might have crossed or circled the park, and passed around or through the arch's open piazza on their way.

Aurelio Ascoli, 1930. Photo courtesy of Aurelio Ascoli

Later, I met Aurelio's friend, Guido Weiller, who was thirteen years old at the time of the beginning of the Racial Laws. He gave me his book, *La Bufera*, (*The Storm*), in which he described the school:

Via Eupili, the two small villas with its newly adapted gym and laboratory, with the shed for the bicycles, with their subterranean dark passage between the two buildings, were completely 'ours.' The outside world was more and more hostile and menacing; we had to gird ourselves to be able to face daily life, to not show up as Jews, to always watch what we said, to avoid, with the most diligence, every situation that might expose us.

But, inside our school we could talk, discuss, exchange news, in complete liberty. And we did it, also involving the professors, who within the limits of prudence, they furnished us, for the most part, ample material to analyze and discuss; besides, the criticism (discussion) of the *Divine Comedy* can be a key to Fascism and Anti-Fascism.

When I asked Aurelio if they had felt freer to discuss politics at this school than they did elsewhere, he told me that my question showed that I knew nothing about Fascism. "Political discussions were not allowed, for Jews or non-Jews," he said emphatically.

The Ascoli family had to fire their maid. He remembers her response. "'I didn't do anything wrong. Why do you want to fire me?' And my mother explained that was the law, because we were Jews, and she was an Aryan girl. It was not allowed. She was so intelligent and so in love with us that she answered in her dialect: 'I will become a Jew.' So my mother explained that was not the point. It was not a matter of religion but of race, the law, the Fascist definition of race. And so, she had to go away."

Some exemptions were granted to Jews who could prove one way or another that they were either not completely Jewish or that their service to the country should supersede their persecuted status.

A few months after the maid left, Aurelio's mother became pregnant, and the family rehired her. Though there were no provisions for this allowance, it may have been that his mother had difficult pregnancies or some such circumstance, explained Michele Sarfatti. Aurelio remembered it more simply: "Pregnant Jews could have Aryan maids," he said.

Aurelio remembered the official card, with one line written in red, telling his mother that she could have a maid. His mother dispatched a postcard immediately to the young woman, who lived in the Veneto region.

"At those times, post cards were delivered within twelve hours. So, that was the Fascists, something good they did. Mail would run in twelve hours. They would have ambulant post offices on the trains, and I remember they stamped the mail on the trains, and in the next twelve hours it was delivered. I'm no Fascist, by the way, but what's right is right, what must be recognized must be recognized."

Aurelio was a particularly aware little boy. He said that was because he heard his parents' conversations at meals; and early on, he was able to read the newspaper too: their maid had taught him to read.

Stories acquire significance because of their place in time. Perhaps Aurelio would not have remembered who had taught him to read if the maid had not been abruptly separated from him. And because his story was part of history too, he could place his own experience within the bigger story, remembering both in that way.

"Everything was heavy; the air was thick," he said, and in that thick air, experiences, like the firing of the maid and the family listening to the radio address, were suspended, as objects might be in a Dadaist's painting, to be pulled out from the frame, looked at, and put back. The retelling keeps them intact, in fact, makes them firm, even rigid. They might lose their life in such retelling and retelling, but these were simple stories full of details, easily entered.

Napoleon's arch, which I passed every day, and the Sforza castle too, began to change: Besides being landmarks, they became characters as well as remnants and evidence of their own times. They were witnesses, and they were survivors.

But Aurelio's memory landscape—his childhood house on Via Bronzetti, the streets in his neighborhood, the school on Via Eupili, and prior to that, the classroom with the Fascist official and the essay—were the places where he could go and get his stories in order to tell them. Experiences seemed pressed like in a sediment, then unearthed by the jolt of sudden association, or by a person asking questions. In fact, they are not stone, but more malleable, and I would soon learn how one Holocaust historian structured her own interviews with survivors in order to avoid the effects on memory of films seen and articles read later in life, long after the events themselves.

Aurelio put his personal stories inside the historical context that he later learned, and once he put the personal and historical together, he told them in complete and intact form. Places, dates, and years formed a structure for remembering one important event. A person seeking Aurelio's testimony for the archive might pull apart the pieces of memory, seeing his story as the way he assembled and made meaning from the facts of his life. For me, this intact story was a part of Aurelio. It was not important for me to determine if the maid loved the family, or needed a job, or both.

His sister's situation propelled a family decision. "She [Aurelio's sister] was born in '22, and in '42, she was [sentenced] to obligatory service," he said. Jews were forbidden to be part of the military, but many were required to do obligatory work instead. Mirella went to work sewing fabric on soldiers' water bottles. She left home at 6:30 AM, to ride a streetcar and a trolleybus from Via Bronzetti to Via Valtelina. Because of the war, food was in short supply, and this, along with the cold winter, caused illness. "They called it jaundice. Now they call it hepatitis A. In those times, it was thought to be a very infectious illness, so she needed to be brought to a hospital."

Aurelio's bar mitzvah that same year helped him to remember the date of the first Allied area bombardment of Milan, which was exactly one week later, during the daytime, on Saturday, October 24, 1942. He remembered seeing the façade of a neighborhood building, Via Bronzetti 5, sheared off by flames. "When we went out of the shelter, the entire building was on fire, and we could do nothing else than watch its collapse."

At the time, his parents were out shopping—it was Saturday, a downtown shopping day in Milan. The maid and his three-year-old sister were at a nearby park on Corso Indipendenza and rushed to their building's shelter during the raid. The maid tried to pretend to the little girl that the fire was a show of some sort, trying to keep her from being afraid. He remembers his little sister "holding her small fists on her eyes, saying 'I don't' want to see the fire.'"

Soon the building cascaded into the street, taking the trees into its flames. He said volunteers were putting out the residential fires, because the professionals had to deal with the sensitive targets: hospitals, military installations, and public buildings.

"All surrounding streets were covered by phosphorous powder from the incendiaries, so the soles of our shoes would be on fire as we walked down the street, unless we kept them wet. There was a small fountain in the Corso Indipendenza playground. I remember a man lifting a little boy with the shoe soles in flame and putting his feet in the fountain to extinguish the fire."

Aurelio's engineer father had been able to keep his job at the Edison Electric Company because his boss, the director, was politically powerful. But Aurelio told me about one particularly tense day in 1942, two days after that first Allied bombardment, four years after the beginning of the Racial Laws.

"And I remember Monday the twenty-sixth, my father coming home for lunch, he sat at the table, and he said, 'Engineer Guastella died yesterday. There will be the funeral today, and from now on I am the only Jew in Edison Company.' I remember this. It was... I can tell you the day, Monday, October 26, '42. Next morning, me and my younger sister were sent to Como."

The general situation in Milan was deteriorating. The Ascoli children went to stay with an aunt there, a one-hour train ride north of Milan.

There was word that another Allied bombing was imminent, and the city and the Fascist leaders, Aurelio said, encouraged people to leave the city. "So, my sister was transported to a hospital in Como, my mother with her. And my father started to look for an apartment for the whole family in Como. It was very difficult to find."

From Como, Aurelio and his father still commuted to Milan, his father daily to work, and Aurelio weekly, to Via Eupili. He remembers doing his homework at their little apartment there, sometimes in the garden, pages and pages of interconnected lessons in math, history, and Latin. He went to Milan every week to demonstrate what he had learned, to what he called an interrogation. I checked with him to be sure the word was what he meant to use. "Interrogation implies some sort of guilt," I said. "Yes, it was like that then. Education was like that!"

The makeshift school on Via Eupili, with fired university professors for teachers, and desks not quite the right sizes—perhaps including the one I used in the archive—anchored Aurelio's week in some sense of normalcy.

At one point during our interview, we took a break, and while Aurelio began the preparation of our dinner, I stood on the balcony of his apartment several floors above the street. He yelled out from the kitchen, giving instructions to look to the right to see the Alps. A warm spring day, the snow-white Alps would have seemed like a mirage, but a fog kept me from seeing them. Instead, I gazed down at the workaday life on the street below and it struck me how heavy with meaning each block, each street, each corner must be for someone who has lived through so much in this place.

We sat again angled at the low table in the living room. Aurelio took my notebook and drew a picture of the family's apartment in Como. They had moved out of their Aunt Alice's apartment into their own small place, and he was drawing it to show me that he slept in the main room.

"Via Mugiasca number 9. Here was the main entrance; here was the hall, not for our apartment, but the whole building. Here were the stairs to the upstairs, and we entered on the ground floor. Oh, by the way, ground floor."

The floor plan would become important later, he told me, but for the time being, we stuck to the chronology. They found a place to live, and, as earlier noted, he and his father commuted to Milan. When I asked him about the mood then, he told me they were waiting for Germany and Italy to surrender every week. Every day, his father would come home from work with another piece of news.

Then things began to happen during that summer of 1943. One piece of news—July 25th, the Gran Consiglio of Fascism voted the Grandi Order of the Day, named for initiator

Dino Grandi, followed by the king's request for Mussolini's resignation. This was the arrest that found Mussolini in secret detention. Much celebration filled the streets as the news got out, but at the same time a heavy cloud of unknowing formed. Some spread word that the war would end. General Pietro Badoglio was appointed by the king to replace Mussolini, and Badoglio announced that the war would continue.

I asked Aurelio how he heard the news.

"The *Corriere della Sera* [newspaper] came out with a title saying, His Excellency the Cavalier Benito Mussolini resigned his office in the hands of King Vittorio Emanuele III. I remember that my father, on Sunday, he woke up, he dressed—don't forget that Jews were not allowed to own a radio. We had a hidden radio in Milano, but we did not take it to Como because it was too dangerous. We were on the ground floor. Anybody could hear us.

"So, my father dresses up as he does every Sunday morning, he goes out to the newspaper stand, comes back. I can still remember. My father was not a tall man. I remember my father entering the door of the apartment with legs as open as he could. Running with legs, he looked like a dancer, like a girl dancer, waving this *Corriere della Sera*... 'Aurelio, Aurelio! Mussolini was obliged to leave the position of Prime Minister!'

"You ask me about the mood, we were mad with optimism, completely out of our minds." Though Badoglio announced that the war would continue, later everyone would learn that he was taking steps toward a surrender, and the Germans were sending more troops into Italy. In this moment, the war might have pivoted, and the surrender come sooner. Instead, a place between possibilities, both horrible and good, was the summer of 1943.

After the family learned that the Italians had signed an armistice with the Allies. Aurelio said, "Optimism left room for worry." Information coming to them in Como was difficult to understand. Everyone was confused. The chaos in Italy would be hard to imagine now, but it was complete. Italian soldiers had no direction from their new leader. On September 16, thirteen-year-old Aurelio was riding his bicycle with a bunch of friends in Como's Piazza Vittoria when he saw a single German tank. He and his buddies circled it, pretending to speak German: hagen spagen, was how he remembered the sounds they made.

When he came home and told his mother about the tank, she forbade him from playing there again and sent him to a place in the woods to play instead. The same day, his sister came home from shopping in the square saying that two German soldiers had stopped her on her bicycle to flirt.

Aurelio's mother called for a family meeting—others of the family were now in Como too—and they all met at his house. Though he would not usually have been invited to such a meeting, he remembered the discussion because his bed was in the living room. He pointed to the drawing he had made in my notebook. He said that his mother thought they should leave Italy, but she was outvoted: the general sentiment of the others was that they were safe. Five to four, the family voted to remain in Como. That was September 16, 1943.

To be clear, and it may have taken a while for this reality to sink in, but the German occupation meant a radical change in the treatment of the Jews. Livelihood and school are terrible things to lose, and second place citizenship is unjust and cruel. But now, with the occupation, Italian Jews were subject to the deportations to concentration camps, to death camps. The Final Solution was under way in all occupied countries. Italy was now occupied.

The next day, his father went to work in Milan, as usual. In the afternoon, his boss, Piero Ferrerio, managing director of Edison Company, got a phone call from someone at the Credito Italiano bank. German officers had inquired after Mr. Ascoli, had gone to his apartment building, and learning nothing there, they went to his bank. Ferrerio hung up and called the engineer to his office and said, in Aurelio's words: "Tonight, before you dine, you are in Switzerland with your family. Do not go back to your office. You take the next train to Como."

Because of Aurelio's evening tour when I first arrived, I could picture his father's trip that day to Como via the train. The office was not far from the Cadorna station, the one whose trains go to Como.

That day Aurelio's father would have entered the station, and then waited at the track for the next train, always aware that he was being pursued by German officers. As I imagined his trip, I felt anxiety, perhaps because I knew the landscape. I realized that I was learning Aurelio's story in layers, as happens in ordinary life. First, he and Liliana drove me around the city soon after I arrived and pointed out his father's workplace, near the station. Layer one was the city, the castle, and the streets, and layer two consisted of my own day trips to Como on the train, from the Cadorna station, walking in, buying a ticket, waiting at the track. Now, another layer, his father's trip from work through the station to Como.

A new swath overlay the station. The whole thing can never be filled in by stories; there is always so much left to know. Eventually big parts of the Cadorna station might seem solid with my own memories and my knowledge of others' memories. Then, I wonder if it becomes just a place again, not anonymous like the first time I was there, but so full of memory as to be too dense to feel it. People like Aurelio and Liliana walk around their city every day with hundreds of gauzy overlays. So many places dense with memory.

When Aurelio's father reached Como that day, the boys who the day before had insulted the German soldiers in Victoria Square had been sent to play outside of the town; they were in a section of Como called the Baradello, where there is an ancient Roman inspection tower. "Now it is a hill with nice villas," Aurelio inserted.

While his parents were arguing about what to do about him, Aurelio came bouncing in looking for water to bring back to his buddies. Instead of filling up, he was told to pack, and to dress in several layers of clothing. His mother was unusually terse. His father had arranged their escape. Filippo Ostinelli, the chairman of the Italian Swiss committee of the International Red Cross would bring them to the Swiss border.

"My mother is cooking dinner, so she turns the gas off, a pot with a roast, and she closes the door of the house, she leaves the keys." His mother told the owner of the trattoria in the front of the building that she could have the food if the family did not return soon.

"At 5:30, we leave in this Red Cross car, which was not an ambulance, it was the car of Mr. Filippo Ostinelli, a Fiat 1100, a black one, so called 'long,' that means not four places, but six places."

Again, Aurelio drew a map with words. "It had reversible, foldable seats between the front and the rear seats, so I remember in the back seats there were my mother at right, my father at left; my older sister in front near the driver; and me and my younger sister in the foldable seats. There were rumors that at San Fermo Della Battaglia—I can show you on the map—

there was a hole under the net. That was only a rumor. But Mr. Filippo Ostinelli must have said so to the driver."

A few hundred meters from the border, Mr. Ostinelli told them that he must drop them off and turn around to go back. It was 6:20 PM, and he had to be back by the 7:00 PM curfew. The family got out of the car and walked toward the border. Aurelio was carrying his three-year old sister. "I had to play the jolly to keep her from crying."

His mother told the guards that they were out for an evening stroll. Aurelio talked about a tall guard, one who remained vivid in his memory, laughing at this explanation: a stroll at the curfew? he asked, smirking. After some game playing, the hole in the border net was indicated by a glance from the tall guard, who said he was in service of the Badoglio government, but they must run because the guard will change shortly. The incoming Fascists would send them back. They ran. They threw their bags and climbed through the hole. His father's bag did not make it. Then they ran again, and when they got to a rock in a field, they all sat. Their fate would be decided by the Swiss.

"There was a small dirt road in the woods and a young Swiss officer passed through this road with his car, with a Swiss flag on the front right fender. He loads all of us to his car. He does not take us immediately to the police; he takes us to a bar to have something hot. I remember having hot chocolate."

The officer brought the family to the town of Chiasso, where in the basement of the movie theater, Sociale, the Swiss Red Cross had prepared and organized a sleeping place for refugees. Every person received a basic mattress and one woolen blanket, which he remembered being more than enough for the hot September night. "Then we got one aluminum cup with cocoa, and two slices of black bread. I ate the black bread, I drank the milk with cocoa, and I fell asleep until the next morning."

The next morning, they had another cup of milk, another two slices of black bread, and then stood in line to be questioned by the police. The Ascoli family was accepted and given new documents. They were the lucky ones: at the time they slipped into Switzerland, the government was accepting the refugees.

The family was loaded into two military trucks, with men and boys separated from girls and women. "And I remember my mother quickly sorted the contents of the backpack, so that the suitcase was with the girls and mother, and the backpack was with my father."

Aurelio and his father were brought to a school in Bellinzona, in the canton of Ticino. The high school was empty because the children were not yet back in school. His mother and sisters were housed in a monastery. "We stayed there three days. So, after three days they took us from Soale and from the nun's college, from then our twenty-two months of Swiss refuge started."

Liliana Picciotto

INTERVIEWS WITH AURELIO ASCOLI and others who lived through the war and meetings with people who studied it grounded those days in an activity I knew how to do: interview. Working in an archive, dealing with what seemed like an overwhelming amount of material, was like steering a vessel toward a known destination but without all the details, or skills, required for navigation: I would get there somehow. If I had given advice to someone in my situation, I would have said that a guide was needed. But instead, I simply asked Liliana if I might, from time to time, interview her. She accepted my invitation and suggested that we meet at the end of the workday at her home, which was a short walk from CDEC.

On the first of those days, I stepped off the elevator and into an entryway that seemed to be in the middle of two sides of the apartment. She led me to the left, through a dining area and into a cozy lamp-lit study, where we sat across from each other.

First, I wanted to understand more about her work. She had devoted her life to studying the Holocaust, interviewing hundreds of Jews who lived during Fascism and the war, including those who had been deported and survived. She searched and dug through thousands of records, in Italy, Germany, Israel, and wherever a story led her. Why?

Sometimes a word sounds more like its meaning in another language. *Per caso* hit me that way when she used it to describe how she became a historian. In English, we say by accident, or by chance: that is what that little phrase means. She chose history and political science as her major in college, and then in her last year, she decided to write her thesis on the Jewish press during Fascism.

Would I be able to see her thesis? I asked her. "It was a first work!" she said in English, her voice running uphill. She spoke Italian and I spoke English. I sometimes responded to her in Italian, and I noticed that when she went into English the words stood out in relief, floating, a surprise cumulous cloud in a clear blue sky, like the *first work*. And the two words fit together so naturally for her, as though everybody had a first work.

CDEC was the archive where she did her thesis research. She explained it had been founded not here in Milan, but in Venice. There, in 1955, several young people began to collect artifacts, various documents, letters and newspaper articles, from the period of the Racial Laws and the war. "It started with a suitcase," Liliana said.

Eventually, they moved their boxes filled with collected letters and documents to Milan, to a Jewish community building on Via Unione and five years later moved to Via Eupili 4, in the former school building also owned by the Jewish community of Milan. First, they took one apartment, then the work spilled into two. The collection grew quickly.

Years later, when Liliana finished her thesis research, and she was still a student, CDEC hired her as a secretary. "But it interested me so much, a passion, incredible. I took over the library." She took classes to learn about running a library, how to catalogue and how to acquire books and materials. She married a young man who had come from Libya and whom she had known from youth. During the period following the Six Day War in Israel, in 1967, they were very involved in discussions within the Jewish community about the war, as well as political activities and discussions boiling around the city of Milan.

For Liliana, there was young married life; then her first child, Letizia; and passion about work. I wondered if one can have this combination of sweet fullness later in life. I imagined Liliana running up the steps to CDEC then out again to attend an evening discussion, hopeful, like so many people during that time, that their groups and ideas would change the world.

I was with her in an interior room, a warm den, a place set up to read or relax. She walked over to a wall of books to find one. "My first real project was this," she said, pulling down *The Jews of Rome,* and she told me to take it. It was her first work of synthesis, she explained, and it led to her next assignment, for which she became well-known. Another woman had been working on a list of all the Jews deported from Italy, but soon after beginning the project she became ill, and the director gave the project to Liliana. It would take six months to complete, she was told.

"Little by little, it became a total passion, so much so that when you go home you continue to think, you still work, and then there was no longer a division between home and work."

Twelve years later, *Il Libro della Memoria* (The Book of Memory) was published. During those years, Liliana worked on other projects at CDEC, always answering requests from the public and fellow researchers. "People like me," I joked, about bothering her while she tried to do her work. "Oh no," she said, "You stay to yourself over there." *Brava di la.*

It may have been brava to her, but I realized the weakness of it. I did not figure out how to regularly ask for help, except for asking for interviews and doing an occasional search for an item. The confidence I had felt while writing up my proposal for the fellowship –a project on paper—slipped away. At first, when I would ask someone about my interest in investigating a particular theme, the person might say something like: "There are many books on that subject." I would go to the library to look at them, and after hours of reading, feeling drained of energy, I would change courses, starting on another part of the project. The synchronicity, that sense of magic that comes early with an endeavor, had been replaced by diligent uncertainty—a discouraging combination.

When I arrived each day at CDEC, I walked into the archive past the long table, which was actually four desks pushed together and facing one another so that it seemed like one workspace, where she and the director, Michele Sarfatti, often worked. There were offices, but they worked at the long table in the archive area, the center of activity, rather than the quieter edges. Maybe they were most comfortable here since they had both started working on the collections, not managing the place, with its needs for funding and report writing.

I slid past the big table, with its occasional guest, a fellow researcher or someone popping in to exchange news. I went farther in, to the little desk that I had been pointed to. No one else ever sat there. I would say good morning or good afternoon and open the shutter covering the window over the solitary desk that looked out to the street. There was enough room for one archival box on the table—sometimes I stacked two, but usually one box took a good amount of time.

At one point, Liliana asked me what I would be doing for them while I was there. I was simply there to do research, I explained, not to work on the archive but to do my research. I felt guilty saying flat out no, and so I offered to think of small projects. I did a bit of research, but not much more. Looking back, I realize that I was extremely guarded with this time I had, not quite five months, to work in a way that I had never had the luxury of working before, without the need to make a living, without my job taking all of my daylight hours, with this project always having to find its place alongside something else. No, I was firm: I was here to do my research. But at least I was *brava di la*.

Until I interviewed Liliana about her own background, we had only met outside her home—at work, at CDEC, in a meeting elsewhere, or in a restaurant—and her demeanor was always businesslike. On a panel or in a meeting, Liliana moved her head from side to side, as a diplomat would, sometimes looking over her glasses, presiding over a convention of peers for whom she was a leader. Here, talking about her family, in her living room, there was a layer of comfort under all that knowledge, and in that layer was warmth. I still remember her dark wavy hair, in the light of the lamp near her. She sank into her leather chair; her usually erect posture relaxed. We were unsure of each other, but she was willing to take a risk on me, which she showed by inviting me to her home.

Liliana's family story started in Portugal. Her father's ancestors lived there until the expulsion of the Jews in the late fifteenth century, shortly after the expulsion of Jews from Spain in 1492, and its then territories, including Sicily, in 1493.

The Picciotto family ended up in Livorno, Italy, a city on the Tuscan coast of the Mediterranean, where they lived for four hundred years. Then they moved to Aleppo, in Syria. Her grandfather's family were cotton merchants, buying and selling Egyptian cotton throughout the Ottoman Empire. They had moved to Aleppo for business reasons, but at some point, after living in a few other cities in the empire, her grandfather came back with his family to Italy, again to Livorno. Members of his family eventually settled in other cities, Manchester and Paris, with one settling in Cairo.

Liliana's grandparents had four sons in Livorno. In 1935, Mussolini, by then in power for thirteen years but still not pursuing anti-Semitic policies, began his explicitly racist program when he decided to invade Ethiopia to make a new Roman empire, to give Italy the ancient luster of the empire. Jews were still called to take part in the army. The mother of the four sons said, no, my sons will not go to fight in that war. The family left Italy and went to stay with their relatives in Egypt.

Liliana ran through the first part, the hundreds of years prior to her own life. Then the story slowed as we approached the war and came to a stop when I realized the good fortune of her family. The Picciotto family had left Italy just in time.

Again, the Ethiopian war marked the beginning of the explicit racism of the regime. Three years after the family left for Egypt, the first of the Racial Laws were passed in Italy. Then the Allied bombardments, followed by and accompanying the German occupation in September of 1943, followed almost immediately by the deportations.

All of Liliana's family survived the war. They had not been living in continental Europe. In Egypt and in England, Jews were safe.

"Amazing," I said, catching my breath in the weight of the moment.

"Yes, amazing," she said.

Her mother's family had a similar history in the near East, and it was in Egypt that her parents met and married, in 1946. Liliana was born in Cairo one year later, in 1947, and one year after that, her parents moved with their baby daughter back to Italy, this time to Milan. The city was a ruin, half of it destroyed. But in the midst of the destruction there was work, and a little girl's future.

Liliana Picciotto—
The Interview Continues

SETTLING INTO A ROUTINE gives a sense of control or order, and so that is what I did. I became accustomed to the arrangement that Liliana and I worked out for our occasional appointments.

We would meet in her apartment after work; a few times I stayed for dinner, and once, we continued our conversation between dinner and dessert. Talking about Liliana's work, her research, was an excellent way not only to learn from one of the most important scholars in the field, but to hear her tell her story. Early on, I did not realize that she too was an important person, personage, in this story, in this pilgrimage I was making. I thought she was a source of information, a person to clarify facts, historical events. I realized much later that Liliana was much more than that.

In the early 1990s, Liliana finished *Il Libro della Memoria* (The Book of Memory). She had found and processed thousands of hand-written correspondence and government records, to come up with a list, names of Jews who were deported from Italy, the circumstances of their deportation, and their fates. A list of people, most of them killed.

"In the early 1990s most of the people did not want to speak at all. In the '70s and '80s nobody spoke, nobody. They came little by little, she said, to speak. Now they speak and write books and go into schools. It was their age that compelled them," she said. They realized they might die without having told their story. When they came around, they did it all at once. Liliana also began to videotape interviews with a hundred people who had been deported, the project that resulted in the film *Memoria*.

"At the same time, a cultural shift occurred in Italy. The story of the individual became interesting to people. Perhaps it was television," she said, that made the individual story as interesting as the epochal story of a group, a political party, or a big idea. "The story of an individual—his suffering and his experience—this era of testimony," she said, "coincided with the aging of the survivors and their need to get the story told." She interviewed people at their homes; then at their childhood homes in Florence, Rome, and Milan; and then she went to Auschwitz with them. All of this took time, and it was emotionally draining for both parties.

Liliana remembered deciding that the interviews would be regimented, not meandering conversations but specific data gathering experiences, each three or four hours long. When she spoke about it, her voice went staccato.

"If you know the history exactly, you can make the questions that specific, and he cannot avoid, he cannot choose. He must respond to that which you have asked him. Then if you ask him, Which morning? How many of you were in the house? At what hour? Who came? What was the weather? What things did they put into the suitcase?... such precise questions, he cannot glide over.

"Therefore, each and every question is so made: How did you got off the train? To the left or to the right? What did you see? What was the weather doing? What did they yell at you when you arrived? All questions are very, very, very precise, and at the end of the interview, very, very long, the person is drained."

"How does the person function after that kind of interview?" I asked.

"They are very disturbed. It is very, very disturbing; it takes some days to recuperate. But it is the only way. We do not want to know only their impressions of today, we do this for the time they are no longer here. Do you understand? Because of the distance in time between when it happened and now, the interviewee tends to introduce things that are not part of their own story: films they have seen, books they have read."

"Si, è vero," I said. Yes, it's true. Sometimes I leave an interview having learned more about the interviewee's thoughts than about their personal history. Because of Liliana's work and that of other historians, the testimonies are for the most part recorded. I can do similar interviews, perhaps, but I am free to ask people about the things that might be considered avoidance or skirting by Liliana. She says at times it was necessary to practically put the person under pressure to make the interviews productive. For Liliana, it was the only way to be sure to get the basic factual information. "It was a very difficult choice, but in the end, a correct one."

If, when these people are gone, we do not have their exact memories, we have nothing. Their memories may have been precise when they were buried inside them, and when they are forced to go find them, they experience their pain again. Someone like Liliana, with her dedication, could do it.

The interviewee must trust her and trust that his memories will be well kept with her. It must be worth reliving the pain, the agony, of seeing a family member murdered, or even just uncovering the first sensation of shame, anger, or sadness the teenagers felt when they were kicked out of school. Talking about the interviews, Liliana seemed suddenly tired, as if remembering them revived the original exhaustion.

"When you interview people in this way," I asked, "do you explain to people that is what you are doing?"

"No no no no," she said.

"You just do it?" I asked.

"Yes, just do it."

"And they just follow?"

"Si si si si, si si si."

"They were very strong testifiers," she said more quietly now. She did not know if they could do it any longer, because they had become older, weaker. They wanted to be available and have the strength to do it in this way.

After finishing the film *Memoria*, she wrote a book for children, one that was used in schools. "A very light, very simple book." She looked for it on a shelf for a moment, then sat.

"I told you that I had four children? This is the baby," she smiled, picking up a picture of Jonathan.

Two children lived in Israel with their own children, and two lived in Milan. Jonathan was an architecture student in Milan. Sara, also in Milan, was about to be married. Before I left, Liliana showed me around the apartment. Her mother lived in the other half of the spacious place.

As our conversation was coming to a close, Liliana told me that a new memorial was planned for Milan. It would be at the place in the main train station from which Jews and political enemies of the state were deported. The Jews went to

Auschwitz, the political deportees and Italian soldiers went to Mauthausen and other camps.

Liliana mentioned a museum being built in Ferrara. There, the history of Jews in Italy would be the focus. In Rome, a Holocaust museum was planned by Mayor Walter Veltroni. He was dedicated to telling this history, and that he went with student groups to Auschwitz. I asked her if she thought all these projects would materialize: At that point, two of the three, both having to do with the Holocaust, were still in the planning stages. Yes, she said, they would materialize. In Rome, the politicians wanted it, so it would happen. In Milan, the memorial might threaten the existence of CDEC. I was surprised by this. In my short association with it, I had already assumed CDEC was permanent. But funding is limited. They would be partners in the research and development of the memorial project itself, and proponents, even though its existence might change theirs.

"We have trouble raising money because people do not see what we do." They were digitizing and putting material online, and that would help, but the memorial would be visible in the mainstream, in the daily commute in and out of the city of Milan. Like so many nonprofit leaders, whenever she was asked to speak publicly, she had to go; she must always be a presence in the public, even if she feels as though she should stay and do the research. She and the director Michele Sarfatti were always working to figure out where to get the money to continue the work.

But their research is the underpinning of all the other work, she said. Without the archive, without the research, the memorials cannot be meaningful, the museums cannot exist. "Nobody understands this," she said.

Liliana Picciotto prepares to give a presentation.
Photo courtesy of Liliana Picciotto

The Boehm File, CDEC, Via Eupili

THE ARCHIVE SLOWLY BEGAN TO REVEAL ITSELF; stories, family heartbreak, and some small but essential victories, like a good hiding place, refuge, a family decision that worked out well, at least for some.

Refuge, the word, implies something temporary, a place between danger and safety, not safety exactly, because it is not home. A place people long for when in danger. Toggling back and forth between my own existence and that of the people whose stories I read in the archive, I found living in a new place, learning its ways, gave me new perspective, like a pair of eyeglasses with lenses that show another layer of life exactly where you are living it.

During the first months in Milan, my apartment was a comfortable, private place removed from the expectations of language and professional competency. It was also the place to begin to experience the domestic part of living here. I had a washing machine with inscrutable numbering on its dials, and a drying rack that opened its metal wings to accommodate hung wet clothing, even sheets. Hand washed dishes went into a rack hidden inside cabinet doors above the sink. This tidy arrangement allowed the water to drip down into the sink while the dishes dried behind the closed cabinet door.

From the dining/kitchen table/desk, looking straight out of the double glass door, a shaft of sunlight sliced straight across the balcony, and ran through the courtyard, the cortile and above the other, parallel, wing of my building. Beyond and above the cortile, the slanted sunlight continued across the backs of a taller brick apartment building and a hotel. From my apartment, looking out to the balcony and to the right, beyond an iron gate, I saw a back alley. There, on the second floor of a house, through an open window, men used a pulley to lower tools and materials to the street. Long slats of wood and unknown objects went down, and other large and small items went up.

Aurelio Ascoli had looked at two apartments and evaluated them for me. He recommended this one, but he said a view to the cortile was second prize for Milanesi: "Italians prefer to look out on the street." At times during the sojourn, I wished I had rented the apartment in the busy tourist district, with people strolling at all hours, but I did like the intimacy of the cortile. I rarely saw the other people who lived in the building, but because of this shared, almost enclosed, outdoor space, I knew the voices of a couple across the way. I liked hearing the conspiring tones of old men talking together below, and the flute of a child who practiced every afternoon for exactly half an hour. On Saturdays, the fragrances of what the neighbors were cooking traveled from their apartments through the interior courtyard and into mine.

A 101-year-old woman had lived in the apartment just before me and it was on the balcony, looking to other balconies in the cortile, that I thought of her. There, perhaps she too had hung her laundry to dry and put flowers in pots. And from the meeting place of sounds and scents, the lives of my neighbors seemed normal, while mine felt suspended.

This suspension, a vague sense of dislocation, permeated the first few months of my life in Milan, at home and in the archive, where pieces of paper, with dates and stray information, had to be rearranged so that I might stitch together the story. At times, such stitching was possible and gratifying; often the results were incomplete, unsatisfying, like a colorful map missing random and badly torn pieces, whole regions absent. Assembling the familiar pieces for structure—knowledge of Fascism's timeline, for example—and for the individual story, an episode, or geographic landmark, became easier over time. And experiences like arranging pots of geraniums on the balcony in the cortile, hearing and seeing life from inside the heart of the building, animated some small details in stories I was reading. That animating was exactly what I had hoped might happen here. I was alone, but everyday tasks brought me closer to this place.

Because of this simple architectural feature, the cortile, I read with a new understanding of a type of space, a courtyard, in the life of a building's inhabitants. But if I felt my life was suspended, in my protected and sanctioned fellowship existence, then Nora Boehm's story of exile, in an essay, and the myriad contents of an archival box, would set me straight.

The Boehm file holds letters, forms, and government documents from 1938, 1946, and 1957, clues about the fate of this family.

A man named Guido Perugia appears as the signatory of many letters in the box, letters sent to various authorities after the war, seeking the final word on the fates of Michelangelo Boehm and Margarita Luzzatto Boehm. But who was he? His name seemed unrelated, but he wrote diligently, undeterred by incomplete replies or blind alleys. The Displaced Persons and Repatriation Sub-Commission wrote that Michelangelo Boehm had been a refugee. And then there was a transcribed interview with Guido Perugia himself, whose own escape from Italy, in 1943, was documented in the transcript of an interview with Renata Broggini. (Her book, *Frontier of Hope*). But who was Guido Perugia? And what happened to Michelangelo and Margherita Boehm?

Then, on September 18, 1945, the Italian Red Cross sent a letter, apparently in response to an inquiry by an Arrigo Boehm regarding Luzzato Margherita in Boehm: Margherita Boehm. There was not anything to report, the Red Cross representative was sorry to say.

One document in the file was titled Scheda Personale. It had been filled out on September 16, 1938, which would have been immediately after the enactment of the first Racial Laws. Completed and signed by Engineer Michelangelo Boehm, who checked yes, that his mother had been "of the Jewish race, razza ebraica," and that his father had been too; and to confirm that he was filling it out correctly, which required crossing out the wrong answer, he wrote next to the cross-outs, "Si" or "No." Yes, he was also married to a Jew; yes, he professed the Jewish religion. Terms like Jewish race, razza ebraica, show clearly the explicit racism of this period.

In1984, Nora Boehm wrote a chronology of family events, which helped me to piece together some of the puzzle. Because of this chronology, it became clear that Guido Perugia was her husband, and it was he, the grandson-in-law, who had carried out this long investigation about the Boehms. Michelangelo Boehm and Margherita Luzzato Boehm were Nora's paternal grandparents.

And in an essay titled Risotto Giallo (the name of a regional dish using saffron) Nora Boehm tells of a visit, thirty years after the events, to the place where, as a child, she had moved with her family to escape the bombardments.

"This summer we were on vacation at Lake Maggiore, and I asked Guido to go to Arona and from there to Mercurago.

"This was the little town that had welcomed us during the evacuation and, therefore, in my memory it remained one of the stages of my life. And this period was very important. It was in 1943, and not only was it a refuge from the bombardments, but from there we fled to Switzerland crossing the lake to Arona and followed first by train and then by bicycle, continuing then on foot to the Swiss border, to escape the Germans who were hunting Jews.

"Mercurago [the town] had remained, despite the drama of the moment, a bright/luminous island with clear memories, tied together with fine threads.

"We lived in a due locali on the first floor, in the house of Maria and Peppo. She, brunette, tall, thin, austere, almost masculine in the line of her face and her voice; he, blond, also tall, with light eyes, without a beard....

"Il Peppo occupied his garden and helped his wife to do the shopping at Dormelletto, that I believe was then very far. Our balcony at the corner looked out at their garden, and therefore I had a way of spying the slow and measured movements while he occupied himself with his vegetables.

"Maria was very busy looking after her little apartment, under ours, and she always said hello to us with a low and hoarse voice.

"Behind the house there was a courtyard, a cortile, that my brother and I called il campiello. In fact, in this campiello, little gracious things happened, exchanges of news and greetings, of gossip above all, calls, and at times also shouts and squalls.

"We called it the campiello of the Marias. Maria here, Maria from there, women with interesting faces, eyes still alive and mischievous, but with bodies of an indefinite form, under ample black skirts and crocheted shawls. Perhaps these shapes made their clothes look like costumes, to us, arrived recently from Milan. In front of the window of our mother's room that looked out at the campiello, there was a slice of the house in which lived our maternal grandparents, Rina and Ottavio Pavia."

As Nora and her husband looked about the place, she found someone who could give her updates on some of the people she remembered.

"All slowly returned to focus in my memory. Not only visually, but also as much the sound of bells connected to that time, to that cortile, to the campiello. The clinking bells of the month of May that announced the beginning of prayers to Maria!

"The house of the post woman next door to ours was there, identical, as then, with the little stairway, pretty and steep, that went from the small room on the first floor. The post woman lived in Arona now; she was still living.

"And suddenly I seem to see Nonno with his paper and his walking stick, trying to pasture two geese, nursed by me with much love. Vira Vira Vira, it was the onomatopoetic song to call them.

"After having found the pleasant memories, I was suddenly hit by the memory of the day of escape: the bicycle, the sacks to put on the shoulder, prepared earlier and stealthily, the silent understanding of every look between mamma and papa, Teddo and me. Suddenly I see again the moment in which I dished out the first risotto of my life. It was yellow, inviting, steaming, but papa said:

"'Enough, we are leaving!' And that way it remained there on the plate in my memory forever.

"Noise perhaps, or the arrival of an unknown person, pulled me from these re-evocations of the past and returned me to the present: Mom and Dad, Sergio and me, we were all saved, and to pause in the campiello meant to relive the escape in the smallest details: to suffer.

"It meant, to re-evoke that which one called the fear of death, fear of being taken by the Germans, fear of wolf dogs that might tear us to pieces at the minimum movement, if the intimidation of the "ALT" did not stop us with raised arms.

"It meant to relive the moment of abandoning all that we had, leaving grandparents Pavia in Mercurago, hoping that nothing bad would happen to them.

"At one moment, returned to the present by noises or unknown voices, I thought, 'Basta,' and decided that to stay longer in the campiello would have meant precious time lost.

"It is necessary to enjoy life, minute by minute."

"Our maternal grandparents, Nonno Ottavio and Nonna Rina would have moved to another town and that way would be saved. At our return, they waited for us happy and smiling and still strong and courageous notwithstanding the ordeals. Together they would live into their eighties.

"They remained living in our hearts and memories: they are no longer, but their deaths were natural, and not caused, as were our Nonni Boehm, by the Germans.

"I gave a long hard look at all of the campiello and a pang in my heart made me understand that I was saying goodbye to childhood and adolescence."

The Boehm file slowly tells the story of Nora's paternal grandparents, the Nonni Boehm, in documents and letters.

An engineer, Michelangelo Boehm had been nominated a Grand Official in 1935 by order of the crown of Italy. A few years later, after the promulgation of the Racial Laws, he was removed from several professional associations, one letter at a time.

Then, in 1947, came a declaration by someone in Zagreb. A Signor Fedor Rozaj said he had been in prison with Michelangelo Boehm, at San Vittore in Milan, and was on the same train to Auschwitz, where they arrived on February 6, 1944. They spoke to one another quite a bit on the train, Mr. Rozaj said.

Finally, a death certificate for both Margherita and Michelangelo. They both died in Poland, it said. *Cause of death: Victims of war.* The more complete story now also appears in the online CDEC archives, and is evidence of much research, perhaps by Liliana. They were arrested on December 13, 1943, and imprisoned, separately, he first in Milan and then at Fossoli, a detention camp; she was brought directly to the detention camp at Fossoli. Margherita's convoy left Fossoli on February 22, 1944; Michelangelo's convoy had already left Fossoli, the month prior. Both were killed upon their arrivals at Auschwitz.

Of course, Nora did not know any of these facts for many years. Certainly, in the campiello and around Mercurago, there was still hope that all were still alive. Nora writes of recapturing memories trapped there—the gauzy ghostliness and then sharp sudden strong but fleeting images of life's passed experiences. We can watch, as though focusing intently on a personal slide projection onto the cortile's walls and corners that only she could see. And the image disappears again, leaving just stone and cement and brick.

The places that we have lived—in the case of Nora Boehm, in Mercurago, with such intensity—what of us do they hold?

"The house was identical, even if thirty years had passed, but other faces and souls had circulated among these walls. I looked out the windows, the balconies, and remained almost stupefied that these inanimate things, but so alive in my memory, might have stayed, restare impassibile, remained unmoved, kept a straight face at my return and did not recognize me."

Shabbat, 2007

THE WEEKEND ARRIVES: No archive, no interviews or Italian lessons, offices are closed, and so there is also a break in my months-long effort to get permission to live here, a *permesso di soggiorno*, which will allow me to get another document with a number that will allow me all kinds of residency privileges, my codice fiscale. These tasks of weekday life are company. So I was pleased when Liliana Picciotto invited me to her home for a Friday evening Shabbat dinner.

We sat down at the long rectangular dining table in Liliana's apartment, eight of us, mostly family and two guests. Jonathan, her son, sitting in the middle of one long side of the table, took a bit of salt, tore off a piece of bread from a loaf and passed it to his left; we each took a piece to eat and passed it on. Dinner was served.

As Liliana's mother watched the table from her end, she sat at a slight angle to it and pulled back her chair, as if watching but also going elsewhere in her memory, another fine place, a beautiful or lively place.

We began to pass food. Liliana's mother spoke French, and her children and grandchildren spoke French with her. Everyone spoke English with me. I started in Italian but quickly slid into English. With each encounter, I was determined to speak Italian, but that resolve quickly dissolved. Eventually almost everyone was speaking English or Italian, including Liliana's mother. The other guest, from Israel, spoke Hebrew, and so at the other end of the long table, Liliana's daughter Sara and her fiancé spoke Hebrew with him. Then Aurelio told a long meandering joke in Italian, and we were all synchronized. Liliana took care of me, passing me dishes of food, and though she did not have one herself, she poured a glass of wine for me.

Sara and her fiancé would be married in June. Too bad I would be gone already, someone said. Sara's fiancé's family was from Livorno, the seaside Tuscan city where they would be married. The couple was huddled together at the other end of the table, already like new parents.

My first Shabbat in Milan, but no candles. The prayer that welcomed Shabbat in my experience was about the candles: "Blessed are you our God, sovereign of the universe, who has sanctified us with his commandments and commanded us to light the lights of Shabbat."

Shabbats at home in Massachusetts started with my friend Diane, at whose house I ate many Friday dinners, with candles. There were usually others at the table, friends, and her two children. She would light the candles and cover her eyes, and I would pull in a deep breath. A few seconds later, when she uncovered her eyes and saw the two flames, something had changed. We around the table had stepped from the week into Shabbat, or at least into the weekend.

In 2004, I met Virginia Gattegno in Venice, and she lit the candle with me before I left. The day had been an important one for me. Before I left, she lit the candle. I began to light candles every Friday. When I met my future husband, the summer after meeting Virginia, I gave him a flat disk set of travel Shabbat candle holders, and in 2007, I took them with me to Milan.

Here, no candles (I learned later that they had already lit them, at sunset), but salt. I like the theater of religious ritual. As a child, church for a time was Jesuit priests wearing robes, with stoles in red, magenta, gold, royal blue, and chalices covered and uncovered, raised and lowered as our eyes followed. Their sermons were delivered to make us think, but it was their theater that I remember most, following their familiar gestures so the mind could go where it needed to go.

Jonathan's salt reminded me of the Christian use of incense, also a ritual of ancient Judaism, and of Egypt and elsewhere. I can still hear the thurible, the censer in which the incense is burned, like a very distant pasture bell. The priests descended from the circular altar and, in a swaying rhythm, swung it out toward the sections of congregation. Scented dust rose over us. The act felt like a prayer on both sides, giving and receiving.

Liliana's mother at her end of the table watched but seemed to look elsewhere, too, in memory perhaps. With husband and baby, she had left Cairo to come here, brushed the dust off their new home, in the ruins of war, and started a new life. When I first arrived for dinner, she said, "Tell me what you have done here in Milan." Then she led me to a settee and invited me to have a glass of scotch with her.

For me, the ritual at Liliana's table would become the lively place that, in the future, I would visit in my mind, while sitting at some other table, or on a train, or watching the night sky. I would see this spacious lit apartment, the settee, the table, Jonathan, Liliana, Aurelio rising to tell his joke. Details would be difficult to pin down: Was it a loaf of bread or just a big piece?

It was a family dinner, talk of a wedding, a grandmother's eyes, the passing of bread, the cacophony of languages—and I had been invited to it.

Graziella Viterbi
—A Second Meeting

It had been five years since I met Graziella Viterbi at the home of her friend Marina Della Seta, with Sally Castelnuovo, a friend of a friend. Though it was only one visit, Graziella occupied a permanent place in my memory, a feeling of generosity more than an image of a face, though the big winter coat and beret were in my mind. Transcribing an interview, going back over the words, becoming familiar with a voice, can keep a person alive in the mind, and in the case of Graziella, her warmly assertive persona lodged itself in mine as though her presence in my life had been greater in terms of time. I knew she went into schools to talk—she told me about it back in 2002—and I wanted to know how she talked with young people. Remember, she had said they were not interested, but she continued going into the schools anyway. I wanted to know more, so I called to ask if she would meet with me again, and a few days later, I took a morning train to Rome.

As I walked toward her home on Via Sicilia, the cool late winter air was already bending toward warmth. The air was light, as was the feeling of being in it. Two flights up a young woman was leaving her apartment. Graziella showed me to her living room and then went about dividing the flowers I brought into two vases.

Spring color, I had requested, and the woman in the flower shop had responded with sure strokes and slices, sliding the orange rose, waxflower, and lily blossoms into a tight and formal arrangement: the high craft of Italian flower arranging. Graziella split it up, disassembling the urban sensibility into to a country field bouquet, changing the very nature of the thing. She placed one of the new bouquets on a table in front of us.

"*Allora*," she sighed, well then, and sat on the couch, facing me and the windows beyond. Her deep voice had not changed: it slid quickly along in sentences, this time in Italian. I was happy to be there with her again, but this time in her own apartment. "I remember the story about how you felt after the Racial Laws, how you felt happy to not be one of them," I said. "That has always stayed with me, struck me as quite remarkable."

As a reminder, Graziella was twelve years old when the Racial Laws of 1938 were passed by the Italian Senate. It was September, just before school was to begin, when Jewish children learned they were to be prohibited from attending public schools, and Jewish teachers were fired. Graziella would not be able to go to her school in Padua. The conversation we—Sally Castelnuovo, Maria Della Seta, Graziella and I—had that day, about the moment that she learned of the Racial Laws, intrigued me, and I thought of it during these intervening years. Graziella told the story again.

"I remember, I was walking in the woods, and I felt happy to be different, to not be one of them," she said.

The first time she said it, this sentence had caused her two friends to wrestle with the idea of gratitude she felt at not being an oppressor. Sally had wanted to know if Graziella had asked, *Why me?* Sally had nearly insisted that she must have asked that question. Both Graziella and Marina had finally convinced Sally that there was no time to think about such things.

"I did not suffer from the persecution. I thought it was the most foolish thing possible. I was happy to not be one of them."

I envied this presence of mind, in particular in a teenager, but also thought such stepping back and seeing the bigger picture could be so useful in dealing with life's indignities, too. She, of course, brushed off my reaction, my admiration of it.

We began to talk about her life now, her two sons, her grandchildren. Soon after settling into our conversation, she rose and walked toward the window behind me. She was talking to someone else.

"Cosa, un gabbiano? Chissa com'e arrivato qua? Poveretto." ("What, a seagull? How did you arrive here? Poor thing.")

"In the window?" I asked, easily lapsing into English.

"No, it is a seagull," she replied in Italian. "One sees more of them flying and arriving in the city, because they don't go back down the river. They never used to come here.

"Come, beautiful one. How did you get here, inside this city, so far from your home? He is beautiful, no?" she said to me. "They come here and can't leave." By now we were both looking at a bird perched on a pole very near the window. She repeated, "He is beautiful. The birds fly up the river into the city, coming into buildings and getting trapped. It is a disaster.

"Be calm," she said, directing her words to the bird. "Oh poor one, you can't find your way home."

She was always waiting to leave Rome, Graziella had told us that winter day five years before. City life was inferior to what she knew in Assisi, the town she would adopt as home after the war, with gardens and people who knew and cared about each other. She wanted to move back into her apartment there, the same apartment in which her family had lived during the war, under the umbrella of the underground movement. She had kept that apartment all these years, returning from Rome every summer with her children and then her grandchildren, too. When her husband died, she moved back to Assisi and into the apartment. Then in 1997, it was damaged by the earthquake, and she came to Rome again. She'd told me back in 2002 that if too much time were to pass, she would no longer have the wherewithal to move back, and that day, Sally had tried to convince her to stay in Rome, saying that she would regret leaving the city just as her grandchildren were growing up.

On this second visit, she told me that her sons, one a rabbi and one an artist, and their children, lived very nearby. Father Brunacci, the family's helper during their clandestine stay in Assisi, who remained her friend during her adulthood, had recently died. And she had just sold the Assisi apartment.

Graziella's phone rang, and she went to the kitchen to answer. She was making arrangements for a trip. When she returned to the living room, she explained that she was still traveling throughout the country to visit schools to tell her story. Often the students were interested, and often they were not. "It depends upon the teacher," she explained. If the teacher was interested and prepared them for the visit, the students were interested. She generally began her talk with a question to students: *What interests you?* They always asked to hear about her personal experience. She still told it often; her story had become like a friend.

Students listened to the eighty-year-old woman telling them about her life as a teenager: the Racial Laws, the hiding, the war.

As Graziella prepared to go to the next school to tell her story, she dealt with a newer problem: the politics of Israel. "When I first began visiting people in Italy in 2000, I did not hear about Israel," but contemporary politics, she and others have said, began to creep into the conversations about the Holocaust. She would tell her story, and often during the Q&A section, a student would ask her to discuss the political situation in Israel. The questions, she told me, do not come across to her as evidence of anti-Semitism, she said, as they might for some who see a discussion about Fascism and the Holocaust turn to the topic of current Israeli politics, but she thought people had a mistaken idea of what was happening there. The students were often more sympathetic with the Palestinians, the *Arabi*. It was important to her to avoid polemics in her own talks, to help them discuss the situation as it really was.

"There is a new anti-Americanism too," she said, and she liked to remind students of two things: "There were long periods in which Jews and Arabs lived peacefully and nothing ever happened." In other words, what is happening is not inevitable. And, the second thing, about the Americans: "Listen, if it were not for America, Italy would not exist."

Students now, she said, are more politicized than in the past. Teachers must work hard to offer an unbiased perspective of events, rather than simply passing on the views of their own political party. "Students arrive at school with the politics of their parents, and at school, they need to hear something closer to objective reality." She worried that this type of education was not happening.

At one point in our conversation, Graziella looked toward the window again. This time I knew what she was referring to when she began to speak of the bird.

"There he is. He has returned to us," she said, "and now another one too."

Grandparents from the War

After visiting Graziella in Rome, I decided to continue south to my hometown's sister city, Cava de Tirreni, a visit which, it seemed, fit perfectly with my Fulbright fellowship's founding mission. After the war, in 1945, Senator J. William Fulbright introduced a bill into Congress that called for the use of surplus war property to fund the promotion of international good will through the exchange of students. In the years following the war the Fulbright has funded scholars wishing to do research and teaching exchanges, as well as students wanting to experience a postgraduate immersion in another culture. Cross-cultural exchange for mutual understanding was also the impetus for sister cities to engage in their activities too. I spent a week in Cava, and it was on a train leaving the small southern city, first to Naples and then to Rome, and finally to Milan, that I had time to think about my experience there.

On the train, I let the visit stretch out in my mind, like short stray film clips, still alive with the echoes of shoes on narrow stone streets, the eyes and words of an elderly man sitting at his kitchen table, the smell of coffee.

Often on a train, I open a book or newspaper, and it falls to my lap while I daydream. Such was the case on the train from Salerno to Naples. I had a seat on the sea side of the train, facing backwards, but my eyes were drawn across the aisle, toward the view of the land.

Across from me, an old woman and a young boy were sitting in facing seats. My gaze to the distance, to the land outside the train, would fall, inside, to them, and soon it floated back and forth, between far and near, outside the train to the land we passed, and then inside. I could almost hear them talking but preferred looking at them against the hypnotic gait of the moving train.

In Cava, I had strolled through the evening passeggiata, where beginning at about dusk, hundreds of people of every age migrated to the main square and nearby cafes under stone arcades, some staying well into the night: older men in small clusters; youngsters weaving by on bicycles; a huge fountain's low encircling wall a stone bench, lined with twos and threes, women and men, sitting like birds on a wire, talking with each other; and teenagers telling their secrets in corners, in this case, near a doorway at the top of the Basilica steps.

Patrizia Pisapia and her brother were the twin engines of the sister city committee, and we talked over coffee late that night at an outdoor café just off the main square. Their idea was to make bridges across countries, via cities. The bigger idea was peace. Cava, just inland, was sister city with places in other countries too; groups on such diplomatic missions came and went from this southern Italian city.

Patrizia and the piazza floated in and out of my mind as the train moved slowly. Across the aisle, the woman opened a bag and she and the boy each began eating sandwiches and quietly talking. Her expression was affectionate, her manner gentle, and I could imagine picking up the light scent of hand cream when she moved. I thought of Graziella and Orietta, grandmothers of about the same age. Beyond the woman and the boy, a long line of apartment blocks, and some cement ruins, half covered with climbing vines, marched past the window frames. The boy asked her a question I could not hear. "It is from the war," she said, *dalla guerra.* They ate their sandwiches and looked out the window. The boy opened a book.

Patrizia had introduced me to her father, a lieutenant in the Italian Navy who had been stationed in Rhodes during the war. Sitting at her kitchen table with Patrizia and me, he talked about how his buddy had been killed when their submarine was hit. Our conversation was stilted because he could not hear well, but I tried to ask questions—naturally I wanted to know more about his time in Rhodes. Virginia Gattegno had been deported from that island. But I gave up trying to get my questions across and just listened. He told me he had been assigned to the submarine that day, but his superior had changed the schedule, and his buddy went instead. Now, he lived without the physical ruins of his war in his daily life—his were in the sea—but that day and its changed schedule had become a permanent part of his memory, bookmarked so that he could skip over everything else to tell of it.

Hearing stories from veterans, though I was not seeking it, gave me another perspective of this war.

Dave Resnik, a neighbor from Massachusetts, had lent me maps of the coast south of Naples that this train traced. Sixty years before, his 36th Combat Engineer Regiment had landed in the Bay of Salerno, not far from where I had boarded. It was September 8 when they approached the coast.

He told me the soldiers guessed about the situation on the ground. They had been told of the armistice: Would the Italians be their enemy or their ally? Would it be a walk-on or a battle?

They disembarked first to smaller boats that would bring them to shore. When they reached land, they learned the answer to their question. They were shelled and the beaches and inland ways were heavily mined. The battle was fierce, with German troops well positioned in the hilly landscape.

Now, on the train heading north, the view was calm, with warm weather that would attract tourists. The sunken ships were long gone, as were the German planes bombing the beachhead. Dave said the memory of the war never leaves, that it lives alongside everything else. He did not have the physical remnants of war in his daily life: no monuments, no ruins along the routes of his daily travels, but he did have ghosts, memories.

On the train, I realized the impossibility of keeping a simple view of a place once I begin to learn about it. I heard so much in the old woman's simple response and my mind wandered toward other conversations, all her from simple *dalla guerra*.

In Cava, another couple we had met along the road had invited me into their house to sip bitters, an aperitivo that the wife had made with herbs. It is a custom, she said, to collect the herbs on the same day every year, June 21. The couple became quick friends, inviting me to a multicourse dinner, giving me a lift whenever they saw me at a bus stop. One week in this small city and I was already feeling like it could be home.

As the train rolled into the Naples station where I would change trains, I gathered my things. The grandmother and the boy walked ahead of me and were folded into a crowd going in another direction. A new train would bring new people, new thoughts. I was not ready to let go of my own floating memories, uncovered by the ruins that a grandmother could point to, ruins that had been left there to be claimed by the land with its climbing vines.

A Weekend of Good Friday, Passover, Easter

Dr. Bill Freilich in Milan treated my first-time seasonal allergies. During that appointment, he asked about my project, my reason for being in the city. He was Jewish and interested in my sojourn. When my fiancé, Fred, visited Milan next, Dr. Freilich and his wife, Daniela, invited us out for dinner. My introduction to Bill and Daniela opened doors into the lives of people I'd not yet met, and the introduction to their world began over the weekend shared by Good Friday, Passover seders, and Easter.

Good Friday and First Seder

For the first Seder, Fred and I were alone. Usually, at home in Massachusetts, this seder is a big affair at a table expanded to seat sixteen or so people. Here, we stood over the small gateleg table facing the glass doors to the balcony. Our flat disk traveling Shabbat candleholder took the center of the table, its short white candles, secured with bits of their own melted wax, slightly askew.

It was the first night of Passover, it was Shabbat, and it was Good Friday, and Fred had just arrived for a short visit. We decided to have our own seder, and for the following night, the second night of Passover, join Dr. Bill and Daniela at their Reform community seder at a downtown hotel. Fred announced that on Easter he wanted to go to the Cathedral for mass, which would no doubt be a special service with lots of people.

We cooked and lit our candles, saying the Shabbat prayer. Fred and I had met soon after my interview with Virginia Gattegno, and so my Friday ritual was already in place. Though Jewish, Fred had never lit Shabbat candles before meeting me, and he was happy to incorporate this ritual into his life.

He put together a small seder plate, with parsley, a boiled egg, salted water, and matzoh, and I cooked a little feast of artichokes, cheese, nuts, and fruits from that day's farmers market. We lit our Shabbat candles. We read a small part of the Passover story. In the dimming natural light, we began to eat. But not for long. A few minutes after we began to relax and enjoy our food, a broadcasted voice filled the courtyard and the apartment. Its message was indiscernible. I immediately thought of Mussolini's famous speeches and neorealist films with their broadcast messages. It felt Big Brother-like: eerie. Fred wanted to investigate, and I reluctantly agreed to abandon the table.

On the street, a strange visual silence covered the sidewalk. This neighborhood could be like that. We walked toward the voice, through Piazza Gerusalemme, and into the churchyard on the other side. The voice was indeed coming from the big church there, and its message was a religious one—a chant. A man and a little boy tried to open the church door but it was locked. The man said that he'd never seen this door locked. We stood for a few minutes and eventually the four of us parted ways, returning in the direction of our two homes.

We ambled, first passing a full, noisy bar. Then we saw lit torches coming toward us. We stepped to the edge of the sidewalk and watched about one hundred people process slowly by in silence, one in twenty or so carrying a flame. Some walked by as if we were not there. Others only glanced at us as they passed. Some looked directly at us, intently. Suddenly I felt part of the crowd along a Jerusalem street two thousand years ago.

Christians become penitents on this day, walking as though behind Jesus being led to his death. Naturally, to become the person walking behind the person who they now know has become their messiah, and who was brutally tortured and killed, is to become very moved and sad. Some become angry and there is a tradition of this too. In some parts of the world, men walk with masks, in others with cone-shaped hoods that resemble gothic spires. Here, they wore street clothes and moved in a gentle solemn procession, but I was reminded of the fervor of the Middle Ages, in particular the violence against Jews, who were blamed for the death of Jesus. This strongly held passion about Jews killing Jesus was puzzling to me, even as a child, given that Jesus was Jewish.

We watched until all of the people had passed. They seemed to be inviting us to join them, and by not following, I felt somehow antisocial, or uncaring, like one of the people in the bars acting as though this holiday were nothing special. As we turned and headed home, we saw again the bars and nightlife bubbling out into the sidewalk. We were happy to return to our table, our food, and our candles.

Passover Seder

The next night, Rabbi Rothman addressed a group, sitting at tables of eight or ten, in the grand interior room of a large hotel, not far from the Duomo. The Reform and Conservative movements do not have a big presence in Italy. This rabbi, from Westchester, New York, and his wife, were living in Florence and Milan as Reform missionaries of a sort, or like what might be called supply ministers, available to fill in when there is not a permanent pastor. It turned out the rabbi and his wife had a summer place in Massachusetts, in the town in which I had grown up. We were seated with them, as though we were guests of honor, and, as surprising as that was, and a little intimidating, I enjoyed it.

The Passover seder, he explained, is celebrated in what is a Roman form, its table ritual, its reclining guests. After reading the service and listening to a child recite the Four Questions—including *Why is this night different from other nights?*—attendees at the individual tables held their own conversations. At our table, the conversation turned to problems in Israel. Daniela had been to a forum about Israeli-Palestinian relations the night before, and she was worried that the tone was pro-Palestinian. I asked if it might not be better that Italians could at least talk publicly about their ideas, something we in the United States seemed unable to manage with the situation in Israel. When people stop talking, they do not stop thinking. Is it not better, I wondered aloud, to talk, even if you disagree?

The question was not answered.

Easter

Easter morning, we walked to attend the Easter Mass at the Duomo. Begun in 1386, the pinkish white gothic cathedral, is a centerpiece, an enormous confection, a brilliant illusion of lightness, its marble spires rising in the middle of a generally understated city of buildings with much less froth.

Many pews were open; people were standing around the edges of the back of the nave, watching but not participating. We were able to sit quite close to the altar and watch a group of priests celebrate the mass. Over a font near the back of the Duomo—we could only hear and could not see—a baby was baptized. It is an Easter tradition, and I had forgotten it.

The mass is the priests' spiritual and brotherly experience up there on the altar. That is what Jose Paul Koovanil, priest in training I met years before, in Rome, told me. I had not understood his description, but then at Easter I understood exactly what he was telling me. We were watching the ritual, but we were not a part of it. We were outside of it, and only when the celebrant spoke to the congregation, leading a prayer or giving the sermon, and then with the communion, the taking of the blessed bread, did we join with those on the altar in the ritual.

My experience of church had included masses with more than one priest, but the services were communal, with lay people given parts, even assigning parts; the priest celebrated, but with the group. My mother, originally Episcopalian, then Catholic for a significant period of time, was active in our church, reading her poetry, even designing a liturgy, with the help of a priest. My parents acted in plays, written by a playwright member of the church, performing on the altar. Artists decorated the walls behind the altar. The sensibility was open and even progressive. The cares of the world were the subject of sermons. Eventually, that church, associated with a Jesuit school, was closed by the Catholic hierarchy and my parents explored several protestant sects, landing in one that most suited their brand of religious practice. At that Catholic Church as a young teen, I learned that religion could be an opening to a bigger world and to different ways of seeing. At the time, I did not know how fortunate I was.

Watching the priests in the Duomo brought me back to my own experiences. Witnessing the ritual, a feeling of awe arose in me and then a happiness for them. I imagined a priest's life can be a lonely one. They bowed to one another inside this well-tuned choreography.

But how strange it was to be in a huge cathedral, one of the world's largest churches, with hundreds of pieces of the deepest of cobalt blue and scarlet glass filling the immense arched lancet storytelling windows, with many of its seats empty.

Virginia Gattegno Cipolato
—A Second Visit

SINCE MY FIRST VISIT WITH VIRGINIA, in 2004, I had gone to the Yale Library to watch and copy that interview with the Shoah Foundation's Visual History Archive, the one that she and I watched together in her house. I listened to it several times, and so in some way, I felt that I knew her. I certainly knew more about her than she knew about me, and I was more sensitive to that idea than I had been three years before. Since 2004, she had made the move that she was deliberating about, to the Casa di Riposo, on *Ghetto Nuovo* (New Ghetto Square).

She had said on the phone that she was looking forward to seeing me. Why, I wondered. But I was pleased and remembered that I must share more about myself this time; she was a woman who would welcome stories from my life too.

Along the way, I stopped at a bakery near the square to buy something sweet to bring to her. The flour-dusted place yielded only breads, so I bought the closest thing to a cake and carried it with me to the Casa di Riposo.

She lived on the second floor of the building, in a large, long room. As is usual, the details of the place do not stick in my mind. I remember a small desk, a couple of chairs—because we sat in them—and a bed. I gave her the little cake and she put it away and invited me to sit. Her voice still sounded strained as she told me that she did not yet really feel at home here, but she did appear to be more relaxed and settled than when I met her the first time. She said she'd made friends with an English woman, and she was happy about it. Still Virginia's warm dark eyes and high cheek bones were prominent features.

This time, I told her, I would not ask her to dredge up her story, but I would be interested to know what she thought about how to teach the history. She was a teacher, after all. Besides the impromptu teacher that many survivors became because they were asked to speak to groups of students, she was a trained teacher.

Some students did ask interesting questions, she said, and sometimes she preferred to talk with them about the time after the war. Many times, students asked if she had forgiven the murderers. She told students that she did not see it as her place to forgive for the sake of other victims, but she knew that she did not forgive anyone for the murder of her brother.

She liked to tell students about the heroic woman making the bread. "This seems like a banal episode," she said, but she thought that in such a situation, one person who gives another food is a hero. "Students should know of these heroes too."

I told her I was able to read about Auschwitz after knowing that there had been some courageous people who had rescued and sheltered others. The good do not redeem the bad, but the courageous ones make it possible to live with some hope while learning the truth.

On the other hand, she said, one cannot expect heroism in this situation, and it is folly to look for it. When one lives at this level, it is simple physical survival. But knowing about people like the prisoner who offered a piece of bread to another prisoner at Auschwitz, made it more likely, perhaps, that I would have the courage to act similarly. Perhaps that is folly too.

She was writing poetry, she said. She told me about a poem that she had just written about a seagull. I asked if I might read it, and she walked to her desk to find it. Standing, she read it to me. Then she sat again, and we talked about keeping in touch. We were sitting inside a room, inside a square, inside a city, on the sea.

We said that we would write to one another. When I stood to leave, she asked if I was sure that I did not want a snack, maybe a piece of the cake that I had brought. I was wearing new summer shoes with red ribbons tied up at the ankle that I had recently bought in Milan, rather uncomfortable but pretty. She complimented them, laughing that she did not wear shoes like that anymore. Her voice was hoarse, as it was when I met her the first time. We chatted about clothing, about comfort versus appearance, and about poetry, dance, and writing: things we both loved. I was happy to speak with her about ordinary things and beautiful things. Was this why I wanted to come and visit again, to come out of the other side of the story and talk about Virginia, the person who lived after 1945? It occurred to me that I had come to be with Virginia, to be with the person, not just the interviewee, or the story.

In her videotaped interview, Virginia said something that I thought of later: "I am not a great person, but I can say one thing for myself: Auschwitz did not destroy me." And I think of something else that she told me: While she was there, she wanted only to survive at least one day after Auschwitz. Just one day after Auschwitz, and then she could die.

Once I asked Liliana if people who survived concentration camps had talked with her about how they survived, and she said it was *per caso*, completely by chance. It seemed to me that Virginia's goal, to survive even one day after getting out of that place, might have helped her. She had somehow got through the selections, when prisoners were selected to be murdered, and that was per caso. So much of survival was per caso. But it cannot hurt to think that her goal to survive just one day after getting out may have helped her to forage for food and try to raise the axe.

Guido Weiller

ILAN WAS THE DESTINATION for all my travels. The Milan station had become the kind of place where I thought about something else while walking along the platform into the station. It was becoming home.

Back at CDEC, I asked Liliana if she knew anyone who had been active in the Resistance. It seemed that anyone who had managed to hide or hide one's identity had done so with the assistance of people—neighbors, friends, strangers. In addition, the ones who helped were those who had become somehow active in networks of resisters, including those groups growing in the hills and countryside, and in cities, and even to some degree becoming an organized national force after September 8. The Resistance was a fight against Fascism and Nazism, but as an extension of the concept, including the act of unarmed opposition, there were many people who sheltered those who were being persecuted.

Young men joined after defecting from the newly reorganized Fascist military, and others, including young women and older people, found themselves involved for various other reasons: hiding themselves, helping to hide others, and fighting. Remember the men who brought Orietta's family to that barn, where they had to spend the night before trying to get into Switzerland? It is likely that they were involved in a bigger network. They knew when the right guard would be on duty at the pass into Switzerland. Orietta's story is full of these people, including the priest who got her false papers, who took her dog, who arranged the family's passage out of Italy.

In a book written long after my time in Milan, *Salvarsi* (To Save Oneself), Liliana states that many more people throughout the country became active after the German occupation. The spirit of resistance filled the spaces that had been passive before the occupation. The cruelty and indignity of the occupiers could not be ignored. What had been ignored or tolerated for twenty years would no longer be tolerated. Fascism crumbled. And the categories of people at risk multiplied. Many had children who refused to serve in the military. Liliana writes that those who hide one category of persecuted person are often willing to hide others.

Many books have been written about the Resistance, of course. At CDEC, I found the diary of Emanuele Artom, a Jewish anti-Fascist who kept an account of his experience. But I also wanted to meet and talk with someone who had been involved.

Liliana recommended that I meet Guido Weiller. He and his family members had been involved in the Resistance after the German occupation. I was eager to meet him at his home here in Milan.

The tram ran in both directions in the middle of his street, Viale Monte Nero, and trees in the median, with their spring leaves, gave intervals of shade there too, creating parallel worlds on either side. On Guido's side of the street, a photocopy shop sold film and related supplies; a tabaccheria was nearby. The square block buildings of melon, pumpkin, and umber tones and very subtle art nouveau flourishes, had balconies just large enough to stand or sit.

Only rarely and only in the neighborhood where I lived did I see anyone standing on a balcony. I wondered why that way of viewing the scene had fallen out of favor. Maybe nobody was home. I could imagine that a child might be able to fathom a world where one only saw people on balconies in one's own neighborhood; to everyone else passing through, the woman standing there, or the old man, was invisible.

When I pressed the buzzer to his apartment, Guido Weiller came down to meet me at the door, and we walked into the dark entry hall, which squarely faced a massive art nouveau stained glass window, lit from the cortile behind it. We took the tiny box of an elevator to his floor, and inside his apartment, walking a long narrow hall, we passed a room where his wife was working at a desk. She looked up and greeted us as we walked by. When we reached his study at the end, a young woman with dark hair was waiting. It was clear that my chair was the one with its back to a sunny window at the far end of the room. As I turned and sat to face the two of them, I saw walls filled floor to ceiling with books.

The woman in the room, Guido explained, helped him, a retired engineer, to write his technical books and manuals, and she acted as his interpreter as well. His English was mostly fluid, and he was determined to speak it, but when he needed a translation, she supplied the English words for him. *Come si chiama* or *come si dice* would signal a conference, and the three of us would talk about the words—what do you call it? how do you say?—often in the heat of the story. I enjoyed these word conferences. At one point, Guido's wife looked in to say hello and ask if we wanted something to eat or drink. We all said no, thank you, and she left us.

Well into his 80s, Guido had a squat, strong build. His mind darted from place to place, and even if he did not spring up to demonstrate an action, his liveliness made it seem as though he might. He rolled out his stories quickly, accepting interruptions and questions, while steering the course.

"Come si dice, scappare?" he asked. *Scappare*, to flee: That is what his family did again and again, as it seemed everyone in Italy was doing.

As a kid, Guido lived with his family—his mother, father, and older sister—on Via Moscova, a street that stretched to just about connect two major parks, the Giardini Pubblici and Parco Sempione. Today the street, near to the city center, is lined with apartment and office buildings, many having retail spaces on the street level. One large modern block of a building had greenery growing so thickly in its square rings of balconies that it seems to be a kind of terrarium with living walls. Via Moscova had a different look before the war.

A few days after Italy declared war, on June 10, 1940, the first Allied bombs fell on Milan. For the first few bombardments, when the alarm sounded, Guido's family ran down to the shelter below the building. During the first raid, his sister was not at home, and after the attack was over, she called to say that she was safe. After a couple of bombings, the parents decided on a policy: After the siren, they would dress and get ready to go to the shelter but would wait to hear what kind of bombing it was, and then decide if it was serious enough to descend. If it seemed to be a heavy enough bombardment to destroy a new building of reinforced cement, such as theirs, they would go down to safety. Otherwise, they reasoned, with three floors of *cemento armato* over their heads, they would wait.

After one particular attack in February of 1943, they returned to the building and found part of it was on fire. Guido helped put out the flames with pans of water. They broke a window and threw out rugs and flammable items and, eventually, the flames were extinguished.

On the mornings after the air raids, Guido and his father would set out to investigate the smoldering ruins around the city and check on friends; then they would make their way back home, and, with amazing deftness, it seemed to me, they would move back into normal life. There wasn't much left of normal life, however, at the time the bombs started to fall.

Since 1938, Guido's father, severely limited by the Racial Laws in his law practice, had "worked under the signature of other lawyers," and so made less money. Guido's mother became a translator and interpreter to help the family make ends meet. "For her, the languages were like eating or drinking coffee for you or me," he said. When thirteen-year old Guido and his older sister were prohibited from attending public school they began to attend the high school for Jewish children that had been quickly set up on Via Eupili. The school soon became a haven from the increasingly menacing world around him.

At one point, the children—Guido and his sister—were sent to stay with an aunt in Venice, and shortly thereafter, Guido became ill, and due to a doctor's orders had to remain inside and rest. He was unable to go outside when Mussolini was arrested and imprisoned, on July 25, 1943; he missed the festivity and speculation in the streets that followed the news.

The new leader, General Badoglio assured the world—the Germans—that war would continue, and it did.

Guido Weiller. Courtesy of Contemporary Jewish Documentation Center (CDEC), Milan.

Eventually, the family reunited in Milan. As resilient and daring as they may have been during the Racial Laws and the bombardments, that summer, they reluctantly joined the mass exodus from the smelly, smoldering city, moving into a one-bedroom apartment in the nearby suburb of Binasco. They, like the Ascolis in Como, commuted by train into the city for work and school.

The Allies had made their first European landing, in Sicily, in July of 1943, and their first bombardment of Rome occurred on July 19. On July 25 of that year, Mussolini was voted out by his Fascist Grand Council. Germans built up troops on the peninsula. Italian and Allied officials were working behind the scenes on the surrender. Then, that armistice, announced on September 8th, brought chaos. Now, we can look back knowing what happened next. Many have written about it. Hundreds of pages in one book, Claudio Pavone's *Civil War: A History of the Italian Resistance*, describe the decisions Italians were forced to make on that day—especially men of conscription age—and the immediate days following September 8. One particularly moving account is given by anti-Fascist Emanuele Artom, a young Jewish man who joined the armed resistance after September 8, in his diary.

Some of his buddies celebrated, singing songs in the piazza, in Turin, while false news and desperate attempts to learn the truth about what was happening occupied many. Word of an armistice on Radio London, but what did that mean? German soldiers appeared on trains. British radio appealed to Italian citizens, saying this is a crucial week to get behind the Allies in their fight against the Germans. Artom knew he would enroll in an armed group. Rumors of Mussolini dead. Artom told his mother that he had signed up. He heard that Italian soldiers were being disarmed and arrested by the Germans. He saw factory workers demonstrating, ready to attempt a disarmament of Germans. A well-dressed forty-year-old man advised against it and was met with insults: "We are tired of obeying you middle class borghesi. Twenty years of Fascism is enough!" Then more false news: Badoglio is a prisoner of the English.

This was all before September 10, which Artom writes is a terrible day. German soldiers were in Turin. Real and false news flew but he asks, "What is true? Only that half of Italy is German, half English, and now there is no Italian Italy."

In Piedmont, he reported, one found soldiers' cast-off bayonets and rifle slings. He mused that "the communists are joyous now because the ruling class has cut such a bad figure." All was falling apart, and the truth was that Badoglio had not been taken prisoner but instead had fled with the king to the south of Italy, which was under control of the Allies.

We now look back and know what happened next. At the time, on the ground, even the soldiers did not have any information, and families tried to act with the information they got from the radio and on the street. One thing became clear: Jews would have to hide or try to get to Switzerland. Any young man of conscription age must choose sides, the Germans (and remaining Fascists under them), or the groups of anti-Fascists in the hills, at first loosely organized, and then similar groups in the cities. Remember, the Racial Laws had kept Jewish men from fighting as Italian soldiers. Now, Artom would have to hide, flee, or fight. He knew he would fight. But for many, all choices were fraught with moral and existential weight, not to mention danger: six hundred thousand Italian soldiers were eventually deported to concentration camps. Political deportees numbered thirty thousand. Eight thousand five hundred Jews were sent to death camps.

Artom did join with the Action Party, and eventually took a leadership role with a formation associated with the Justice and Liberty party. In March of 1944, he was captured, imprisoned, and tortured. Within two weeks of his capture, he died. We are fortunate to have his writing, which tells so brilliantly of the moments in which he lived.

Guido Weiller, though curious and alert, was younger and, at the time, not politically inclined and perhaps not as politically aware as Artom. Still, he remembered similar confusion on September 8, beginning with the sound of a man yelling in the main Binasco square: "La pace sia con noi!" (May peace be with us!) Then, the bombardment refugees like his family—the town was full of them—put their heads together. What could this strange language mean? Soon more news came, but not less confusion. Radio London reported that the Italians had signed an armistice. Soon after that, defecting Italian soldiers began to appear in the town looking for civilian clothing. What might have been a day or week of joy was turning to a time of foreboding.

In the midst of a broadcast that followed, this one in German, Guido's father turned off the radio and said, "We must go." Binasco was on a main road and train lines, and just as important was the fact that everyone in town knew the family was Jewish. "One cannot be a Jew with the Nazis," Guido said, matter-of-factly.

The family looked at maps and the next day left with two suitcases and two backpacks, walking from their apartment, and under orders from their father not to greet anyone. They did not want to have to explain or be delayed. They took a train to another smaller town away from the major modes of transportation, off the beaten path, and they thought, safer.

After a night in a town that was too remote and outside of all communication, and then one night in a town not remote enough, the family decided to stay in Quarna Sopra, between Milan and the Swiss border. It was there that Guido saw, for the first time, women carrying chests of wood, fruit, and chestnuts on their heads, and, always curious added that he had asked how many kilos they were carrying: twenty was the answer. "That's heavy!" Guido exclaimed to me.

It was hard to keep Guido on track with story that I had come to hear: How did it happen that his family joined the armed Resistance? Instead, he would jump forward to his career after the war, telling me stories of his engineering work in twenty-two different countries.

One time, I listened rather impatiently while he talked about how he was sent to Brazil to fix a problem with the major mass transit system, using bits of solutions and technologies available there. Sociologiest Claude Lévi Strauss had called this type of work bricolage: making something from almost nothing. The same sorts of stories happened all over the world for Guido in his later career, and it seemed that he was going to tell me about all of them, but I had come to hear about the Resistance.

Only later, listening to the recording of our conversation, did I realize how wrong it was to rush him back to the war, back to Val d'Ossola. It was all related—all one life—and so what did it matter that it came out of order or took many hours? I did not realize the rich connections in the story. And what about our kind interpreter from Trapani, on the west coast of Sicily: What stories might she have told if I had been more generous with my time and curiosity? I was trying to separate out one period, one epoch, but this was a person's life, not just an epoch, and he wanted to talk about it. Guido was a bricoleur, a resistance fighter, and then an engineer, and if I had realized that fact during our conversation, I might have participated more in the storytelling and learned something different.

But to the war we returned, and to the details of his family's escape. In the small village of Quarna Sopra, the family eventually found a little apartment, with two bedrooms. They moved in with their suitcases and backpacks and waited. All ears were leaned toward broadcasts of Radio London. Allied bombings continued; black markets thrived, food was scarce, and the northward movement of the Allied troops was excruciatingly slow. One Nazi raid, and they could be deported.

In Quarna Sopra, soon after their arrival there, Guido saw a transport of goods passing in the street and heard that it was headed to a partisan encampment not far away. Another day soon after that, a man in the square yelled, "Germans!" and the family hid, until a subsequent yell announced that it had been a false alarm. When the family regrouped, they realized that their Jewishness was known, that the town seemed to be at least somewhat organized against the Fascists and Germans, and that the nearby partisan group in the hills was somehow related to that organization.

Guido wanted to introduce himself to the head of the group. After checking with his parents, he approached a man who was eating his lunch in a café. He knew his name was Beltrami, and he had heard that the man had been an architect in Milan. Beltrami offered assistance to the family. Part of his job, he explained to Guido, was to protect those persecuted by the Germans and Fascists, including Jews.

A few days after that lunch with Beltrami, another transport passed through the square, and Guido realized they might be able to use a volunteer to help to deliver the food and supplies to the partisans. He ran back to home to consult with his father. It would be a dry run, he said, a chance to check out the partisan camp. Given permission, he ran back to the square to pick up a pack and hike along with five other men.

When he arrived at the encampment on the mountain slope and deposited his pack he asked if he might be able to join them at some point. He was told yes, that if he were to decide to do so, he should approach the camp, and at a certain spot on the road, yell "Quarna!"

While Guido was becoming familiar with the partisans in the hills and his family was embedding further into the countryside of Northern Italy, violence and chaos of occupation gripped the German-occupied country. Alessandro Portelli, in an oral history of a massacre in Rome—*The Order Has Been Carried Out: History, Memory, and Meaning of a Nazi Massacre in Rome*—recounts one month, October of 1943, showing the utter state of violence that pervaded that city, violent actions against civilians, actions which he said were not precipitated by partisan or civilian action, in this paragraph:

> On October 7, the Germans arrested and deported 1,500 carabinieri; on the sixteenth, they raided the Jewish ghetto; on the twenty-seventh, one thousand people were rounded up in Montesacro, and one third were sent to forced labor. The war against civilians was raged relentlessly, with a sequel of roundups and mass deportations all over the city. Many deportees would never return. None of these acts was related to partisan action.

Things happened quickly that autumn. On November 30, the Fascists, now set up with the released Mussolini in a puppet government under the Germans, announced that Jews were to be considered the enemy, that their goods would be confiscated, and they would be sent to concentration camps. Suddenly, the family's situation was even more precarious: Italian officials who remained in their jobs, now working under the occupying Germans and puppet Fascist government, had new orders from their own Fascist leaders to participate in the arrests of Jews. This time it was his mother's decision: They would approach the partisans to get their protection. In a book that Guido had written, and which he gave to me that day, he describes the moment of her decision: "We must leave. We will eat, pack our bags, bring a cover for each bag, carry with us a little something to eat."

And so, the Weiller family left again through the back door, so as not to see or greet anyone, and walked the same path that Guido had used to carry supplies to the partisan camp.

The Partisans

I later went to Guido's book for a description of their first days in the place. A little village of summer shepherd houses situated on the edge of a chestnut forest formed the encampment of Camasca, and the family was given one of the huts. That evening, they ate their first meal there, a little meat and a few ravioli: the food they had brought from Quarna. There were two glasses to share among them, and a few metal plates. His mother gathered leaves into piles and placed the coverings they had brought over them for sleeping.

They lit a fire and watched it in silence. It caught something and spread into the room; his mother quickly stamped it out. Then she began to cry. In his book, Guido describes seeing her—illuminated by the flame, "her tears unstoppable." In his memory, it was the heaviest moment of that entire period.

I could imagine her exhaustion. Through all my interviewing, I was meeting people sixty years after the war, people who had been children and teens at the time, whose parents were now gone. I knew that the memory of a teenager like Guido would have its own significance, could not be that of an adult. I could only imagine the horror of not being able to keep one's children safe. He could not talk about what she felt, and he could not know, but he could tell of the decisions that his mother and father made, and he could tell of her tears. The rest of what we might know about her generation would be found in boxes in the archive, collected when the parents who had survived were still alive. I was grateful for his memory of his mother because even after following all the movement of the family, I did not have a sense of her, aside from her courage and her own bricolage, the interpreting and translating to make ends meet. Now, finally, in Camasca, after the bombardments and decisions, and moving and more decisions, and maps and trains and more decisions, I saw her as a mother, and she was crying.

That first night in Camasca, they did not sleep much, but when morning came, eighteen-year-old Guido had his eye out for the activity in his new place. Soon he approached the assistant commander, Lino, to ask to work. At first, he was given small tasks, to make a survey of the camp, then to act as a courier, preparing and sending messages to and from other formations and to members within his own group, which he said eventually numbered about 120.

Guido graduated to working on a pile of old guns that were encrusted with dirt and missing parts, and at a rate of one or two per day. Guido got some of the guns into working condition. "I was clever with my hands. Then I learned to build and make mines. An expert came down from the city and he taught me how to do it."

Guido made a whistling sound to fill in words: "I had my se se se se se se, how do you say, so I could build it. Someone came from the valley with a message, a biglietto, with a signature I knew: 'I want one mine, two mines, three mines.' I could do it. Da dada da da, no problem." He was not always fighting, he explained, but his group was bent on impeding the Germans and the Fascists.

One dark night, Guido and five others were on their way to blow up a Fascist unit when they saw a truck full of soldiers approaching them. "We destroyed it and pushed it into a nearby lake." But before pushing the truck into the water, they took the shoes off of the dead soldiers' feet. "*Come si dice, scarpe?*" he asked.

"Shoes," his interpreter answered, her contralto voice sure and kind and her English carrying a soft lilt.

"Shoes were always a serious problem with the partisans," he said.

Whenever I was impressed by a story and somehow expressed it, he would tamp it down. "Interesting," I would say.

"Not interesting!" He said: "You see, when things are so heavy and so quick, for every day there came something else, something new, there was something to do or to plan. You don't think your way of living is so strange."

Eventually Guido's father became the group's cashier, and his sister worked as a nurse: The Weiller family from Milan, a lawyer with children bound for university, was instead working alongside the armed resistance, and, through the winter, living in a summer shepherd's hut in the hills of Val d'Ossola.

At this point in our conversation, Guido began to speak as if he had become more or less an independent agent. He mentioned his family here and there, but he seems to have become completely involved, at least in looking back on it, with his work and with his group of colleagues. The characters: Beltrami, Lino, escaped English soldiers, a partisan girl from another group. They were his university.

One afternoon, Beltrami called a meeting and introduced a person wearing civilian clothing, a representative of the Comitato di Liberazione Alta Italia, the group that took charge of the organization of the northern resistance, formed from the Milan branch of the larger organization, the Committee for National Liberation (CLN). Guido guessed that he had come to lift morale, and it worked. He told the group that they were a part of a connected network of groups like theirs, which operated throughout the Alps and Apennines. Another band of groups, called GAP, operated in the plains and cities. And a Brigata Italiana, Italian soldiers in the Allied occupied south, had been inserted into the Allied Eighth Army. Now, a full explanation of the groups would fill pages and include political party affiliation and philosophy: communists, socialists, Catholics, etc. But that day, Beltrami ended his talk saying: "We don't have typical military supplies or provisions, but we must damage the enemy in any way possible."

Guido explained what that damage looked like. One day, he went to a hydroelectric plant two thousand meters above sea level and clipped some wires. The purpose? A group of Germans would have to come, thus taken from some other activity, and figure out what happened and fix it. We could stop them for a day, two days. Everything was dark, and so the factories stopped. "This is the partisan war, and we could stop half of the Milan industry by acting here." Of course, industry was now being used in service of the occupiers.

"Night night—not sera—not evening," he explained, was often their time to work. Like the night they destroyed the German truck and took the soldier's shoes, their task was to keep the Germans and Fascists watching their backs, fearing for their lives.

The partisans were "like a bee buzzing sound," he said. "Fighting with strange methods, but fighting, and this is what I lived."

Portelli talks about these buzzing bees in Rome, though not using that term. In Portelli's book, Mario Fiorenti said their work was to keep Germans feeling they were not the masters of Rome, that they are amid a hostile population. "We would attack their communication lines, their transits, their truck routes, the truck stops, their headquarters, and especially this: they were not to march with impunity through the city." They also created traps with nails that punctured Nazi soldiers' truck tires, leaving them vulnerable to Allied air attacks.

The Girl in Lugano

In the region around Camasca, Guido was assigned to guard the funeral of a member of his group. Armed, he and others spread out along the route of the cortege, just out of sight, in an area known to be thick with Fascists (Repubblichini, or Fascist after the fall of Mussolini). He waited and watched as his friends passed in silence. Any moment could be massacre, and Guido knew that their ammunition would probably not hold.

Nothing happened, but the experience hit him: "A partisan, when he works, is completely isolated from his base, and in many cases, there is so often no true and proper base". A funeral, in war as in peace, allows a certain space in the mind for reflection, or at least an awakening to one's own limited time. Maybe that funeral was the reason that in March of 1944, when Guido got sick with a fever, he decided to cross the Swiss border. By this time the rest of his family had already left.

Guido did not talk about how it felt to leave his fellow fighters. Perhaps his more or less incidental reason for connecting with them made the decision easier—we do not know. He was ill and decided to try to head to safety. And his leaving did not mean inaction.

Guido's escape into Switzerland was easier than any story of this route I had heard or read about, maybe because of his familiarity with the contours of the land and experience living in it, maybe because that is how he remembered it. "For me it was very simple, for there was the forest, and we went through the forest, then I found a piece of—*come si dice, pietra*—stone, and so we are in Switzerland. I don't remember passing the border."

Guido ended up in the Italian section of Switzerland, in Lugano, while the rest of his family had entered another way, and they were in Lausanne, the French part. He was sent to an internment camp and was enrolled in a school there.

"I was alive, working; I was studying; I had something to eat; and after, I had to act. I was one of the older ones," he said. "We worked and we did what it was possible to do, and possible to do is to get arms into Italy: people and weapons."

He tried to explain the base of their operations there. "There was a very big cellar, and this big cellar was in galleries; the Swiss personnel didn't know we had [things] hidden [there]. There was a strange big house with a park, and under this park there were, I think, seven or eight galleries, one kilometer of galleries, and there in these galleries we had put persons, weapons, arms, everything. I was charged with making the heating and hot water system work."

"So it was like a station," I asked.

"Yes, like a station. But the Swiss people never knew. They didn't think that we boys could make such a thing. Sixteen years old, over to and fro [over] the borderline, with persons and weapons and arms."

One day before dawn, Guido was awakened by one of his buddies and a wounded girl. He woke three others who opened a gallery with light and heat. They held a roll call, and then he went to find a doctor, whom he brought blindfolded to the wounded girl. "Morning and afternoon, he came se se se se se [whistling sound], blindfolded, two times a day. After I think three weeks, the young girl was walking. We took her on little walks. I remember that this girl, I met her five or six years later in Florence, and she was very, very quiet, married and with a baby."

Guido's story of the partisan girl turned mother after the war reminded me of a recent conversation with my friend Giovanna Brunelli. We were walking through the miles of porticoes in Bologna, enjoying a day off, strolling and catching up, eating gelato. We veered off the main streets. "Right here, Marco Biagi was shot." She was referring to a murder that took place in 2002. He was a jurist and advisor to the Ministry of Labor, led by a conservative of the Berlusconi government, and he was involved in the regulation of labor. In the period, perhaps even the week that we were walking through the spot, a bill was being considered, she told me, that utilized his ideas for economic development. He was shot by the Nuove Brigate Rosse (New Red Brigade).

She talked about the terrorist bombing of a train in the Bologna station, where eighty five people were killed one hot afternoon in 1980. That was the work of a network of right-wing terrorists.

The postwar political situation was gestated between the world wars, during Fascism's rise, and then in hills and valleys like Val d'Ossola, and in Switzerland, and precipitously by the forces and governments outside of the country's borders—including the postwar anti-Communist Allied occupiers. Giovanna's casual stories in Bologna that day told a part of that story. And apparently, after the war, the girl partisan in Guido's story, became a mother with a normal life, but after twenty-two years of dictatorship and then war, what is normal? How long does normal take?

The war's memory extends into our time, into the life of my friend Giovanna and everyone who lived through the postwar terrorism in Italy. I wondered how war's memory might live in a country where the war had not been fought, like in the United States. Giovanna's uncle was a partisan in the hills in Umbria, and she had books that included stories about him. In the US, we had only polished stone memorials in town squares. As a child, the monuments meant little to me. But if an uncle had fought a few miles away, in a hill I could see from my school, might I think differently of war? I had changed trains in that station many times—Bologna is a train hub in Italy—and I sat in the waiting room, the room where the 1980 bomb exploded. Being there in the station on the way out of Bologna that day felt different from all the other times I had passed through it.

Of the various shades of resistance, historian Philip Cooke named two types of resisters: those who harbored anti-Fascist feelings over a long period of time and even acted in the first days of Fascist activity—and throughout the dictatorship—and those whose opposition to Fascism developed during the war. Liliana's book *Salvarsi* mentions another resister: the one who saw the first weeks of German occupation and decided to act. But, regardless of political affiliation, it seems most people went along with their lives during Fascism and the dictatorship as best as they could, adjusting to this indignity or that hardship. Their resistance was activated during the war and then the occupation. Liliana talks about the sudden waking up of a people who had been living under dictatorship. In the early days of the occupation, they saw the arbitrary and meaningless violence and hatred of their occupiers, and they became resisters.

But resisters acted in the early days of Fascism, too. Portelli documents two battles in the neighborhood of San Lorenzo, in 1922, when Fascists were coming by trains to a big rally in Rome, when "the people of San Lorenzo took to the streets [with every form of real and improvised weapon] and pushed the Fascists back."

Natalia Ginzburg's *Family Lexicon* tells of her Jewish family in Turin, where anti-Fascism was the in-house language and its action outside, too. Several of her family members were imprisoned for their anti-Fascism early on. Her husband, Leone Ginzburg, also active early on, was tortured and killed during the German occupation.

Carlo Rosselli, a Jewish intellectual from an affluent family, fought for liberalism and socialism, was a devoted anti-Fascist who created the Justice and Liberty party, and was forced into exile in Paris, where he published anti-Fascist literature and set up a network in Italy for its distribution. Eventually, he and his brother were murdered in the French countryside. The stories of these intellectual and proletarian anti-Fascists inspire. In 1924, after an election fraught with violence and fraud, a socialist member of Parliament, Giacomo Matteotti spoke in the Chamber of Deputies about election regularities. Less than two weeks later, he was found dead, murdered while walking along the Tiber River.

By the time of the German occupation, many anti-Fascists, Jewish and non-Jewish, were in exile. In Switzerland, in 1944 and 1945, the Weiller family and all of those who had managed to get across the border, were waiting and planning for the day when they could return home. The day came. By late April of 1945, the Germans were leaving.

Guido said his group had inside information: "Get into Italy as soon as possible, because the Americans will close the border." There was a train going to the border from Lugano. "When I was leaving, I was on the train, someone from our organization came and gave me a big envelope, and told me, 'Now as soon as possible, you go in Milan to the highest grade you can of the new Italian anti-Fascist organization. So, I looked and there it was, the photographic documentation of Auschwitz."

When he arrived in Varese, just across the border, he found someone who gave him a motorcycle that he and his two buddies were to use to deliver the package. "In this auto route, there was not a man, not a cat, nothing, only we saw over and under, the German army going to Germany. It was dangerous, and we had nothing."

"In Milan, it was impossible to move anywhere. There was shouting: Piazzale Loreto, Piazzale Loreto. What is Piazzale Loreto? We didn't know. We went to Piazza Loreto, and they had hung Mussolini and his mates."

"Quite a combination of images," I interjected. By now I should have known better, but I could not stop myself from saying it. This time he agreed.

"Yes. Yes. The day after, I went there, and there was fighting, a house where the Fascists stayed, and the partisans. I asked one of these partisans, "Where is the headquarters?' 'I think it is in Piazza Della Scala,' and there I found the headquarters in Piazza Della Scala. And I went to someone, I don't remember the name, and he was amazed. Nobody had an idea of the concentration lager, and so my mission was done."

Then Guido went to his house to see what had happened to it. He found a German, who said he was not a military man but a businessman, living there. "I told him to go away, and I entered my house." Their home had included his father's office and was spacious, and Guido filled it up with six other partisans. Eventually his parents and sister returned. "And this was—you see, I am alive, my parents are alive; I have a house—this was very important after the war."

Guido even had a job. He knew English and was offered a position on a newspaper. But he did not like the schedule, even though it resembled the schedule of Camasca: working late into the night. "You came back home at four o'clock in the morning, and also only rush, rush, rush, write, write, write. I didn't like it." He decided he would study engineering, as his grandfather had done.

"My father told me, I can give you a house and food to eat, but I have no money." So, Guido wrote for the newspaper to finance his education while living with his parents. He got his degree when he was thirty years old. As an engineer, he continued to write. He went to the shelves and pulled out the technical books that he had written.

He searched the bookcases for the map that would show Val d'Ossola, and finally found it, and together we looked at his world, from Milan to Omegna to Camasca to Campello to Lugano and back. Not to mention twenty-two other countries. "When I see a place on the television, I say: I have been there!"

I was ready to leave after almost three hours of listening. Guido seemed to want me to stay. If I had been more relaxed in my approach, if I had simply stayed until he wanted me to leave, what might I have learned? Instead, I write with some regret that I left Viale Monte Nero on my own terms, a bit early, and headed straight for the tram to go home.

It was spring in Milan, sixty-five years after the events that Guido had described. The flowering trees in the median were green. His memory and his words had brought us to the winter of 1943–1944. Guido had constructed his story to fit inside an interview, to fit into telling form. The parts were there, without some of the less stupendous days of more ordinary memory gluing them together. In rapid succession, he told his life's events in a string of stories. After listening to Guido, stepping out into the street again, I was in the city of Piazzale Loreto, of Via Moscova smoldering after bombardments, a city whose names have multiple meanings, where Piazza della Scala meant more than the square with the famous opera house.

Guido's story by itself gave a view to the inside of an unknown world, a partisan group in the hills, an embedded reporter, and more, a participant. This was just one piece of a complex story about the war that was defining life in Italy. Piecing together fragments again. Someday in the future, Alexander Stille would recommend the book about this civil war, by Claudio Pavone, with clear chapters on aspects of the Resistance, and my searches would yield other less comprehensive books. But my familiar way unfolded again, one story, then another, slow and plodding. Now I look back and question this method.

Why was I working on such an immense topic, one that grew in a new direction every time I learned a new part of it? The Resistance is a subject that deserves a lifetime of study. How tempting it was to retreat, to sit on the bench in Piazza Gerusalemme and watch children play soccer, write dreamily about life in Italy. But I was there to work. I had received a Fulbright fellowship to do this work, and so I comforted myself with my house on the square approach, putting my attention on the individual stories. Eventually I would begin to understand what had happened. Guido's story was a new lookout from that imaginary house on the square.

Olivetti

Another story had been unfolding for me over the years, that of Camillo Olivetti. His story came to mind when I heard about Guido guarding the funeral procession of a fellow partisan.

I had just read about the funeral of Camillo Olivetti, founder of the Olivetti Typewriter Company. Back in 2001, the Olivetti

Foundation awarded a grant for the Lenox Gubbio exchange. By the time I interviewed Guido Weiller in 2007, I had met three of Camillo's grandchildren: David in Connecticut, Philip in Ivrea, and Laura in Rome. Laura had loaded me up with books about the family, one of which was a collection of letters written by her grandfather, a small, beautiful paperback in a slip case, a collection of letters to his mother and to his sweetheart, *Lettere Americane* (American Letters).

After graduating from the Polytechnic University, Camillo traveled to England and to the US to study industrial practices. During one American trip that lasted a year, he travelled by train and by bicycle, noting the civic and social life in the new and strange country. He wrote many letters home, one about the Chicago fire department, whom he shadowed, clocking their response time to a fire; he interviewed Thomas Edison in New Jersey; and for a time, he worked in an empty lab in the not yet finished Stanford University.

Back in Italy, he founded his company in the town of Ivrea, in the Piedmont, a region known to have been important to the formation of Italy, the Risorgimento, unification, a long process of revolution in the middle 1800s. The Piedmont's own Camillo Cavour is one of the Risorgimento's protagonists. Jews were disproportionately involved in the revolution, as compared to the rest of Italian population. For them, it brought complete equality. Soon, Jews could aspire to the highest levels of government.

Camillo Olivetti was Jewish; the woman he married was a Waldensian, a small sect that predates the Reformation. Camillo, himself an industrialist and a socialist, whose views of socialism were evolving, was attracted to Unitarianism and, at one point, he converted. By the 1930s, his company had businesses in several countries, and his son Adriano was rising within it.

I was struck by this socialist-industrialist combination because our American system does not seem to allow for it. Camillo believed in the equality of what is considered manual and intellectual work and said that manual work is of course intellectual. He rode his bicycle everywhere, and to stay warm, for insulation, lined his clothing with newspapers.

While staying in Milan, I went to Ivrea to meet Philip Olivetti. He took my fiancé, who was visiting, and me on a tour of the company site, to see buildings created before and after the war.

Adriano had been especially interested in hiring the best architects and so the buildings were iconic and individual. The company had an early company-based childcare center; one of the buildings housed a library, and a huge terrace encircled it, a place for a rest in the open air after lunch. This was how people in the area lived, and that lifestyle was incorporated into the company.

Camillo had designed their first factory building in Ivrea, but their sites in town eventually included industrial structures designed by leading architects. Adriano's views, often called utopian, were reflected in the design.

When Camillo's son Adriano was rising in the company, both were involved in anti-Fascist activities. In a well-known story about the escape of a socialist wanted by the Fascists, the names of both Adriano and Camillo come up. The Olivetti Typewriter company was known as a "most important center" of anti-Fascism, according to one record dated 1934, in the State Archives. Camillo was an outspoken writer on political affairs, and he was a Jew, and during the German occupation, he had to find a place to hide. He found refuge in a small town named Biella. He became ill and died there. Another secret burial, and for this one, we are fortunate to have a witness, someone named Bigiaretti.

"It rained the day in which he was transported to the cemetery; but from Ivrea, from nearby small villages, from various places in the Canavese, the workers were making their way, hiking, *su per la serra*, to Biella. They arrived by every possible mode, most by bicycle, at great risk and with great effort. The Germans had just hunted out and terrorized the entire region. The little Jewish cemetery of Biella could become the site of a massacre, *il recavisi una sfida temeraria*, a daring challenge; but they came to him that day, silent men, heads covered, and on their faces, the rain cancelled the tears."

Meanwhile, Camillo's son Adriano was in exile in Switzerland and, for the second time, in communication with the Allies. The first time, before the armistice, his attempts to communicate became known and he was imprisoned, to be freed during the chaos following the armistice. In Switzerland, he worked on his plan for Italy's new way forward. He would become a national figure, a senator, and known for his utopian ideas. Many biographies of Adriano exist, and one of his proponents, a biographer, Davide Caddedu, was surprised, when I met him in Milan, that my interest fell more on Camillo. I could not help my fascination with the father. He was a character, a man of action, and it seemed to me, he was fully engaged in life. But most important, he started a major company with a particularly thoughtful founding and existence.

Camillo was a national gem, and he had to die in hiding and be secretly buried.

In 2022, CDEC produced a podcast about Jewish Italians and the Resistance, *Resistenti Ebrei d'Italia*. It is an important contribution to the scholarship and to popular memory. It can be found on their site.

Liliana Picciotto
—The Deportations

ALL THE STORIES ARE URGENT because we know that for the Jews who did not manage to find a place to hide, or manage to get to Switzerland, to obtain false identification and live as non-Jews, or join a partisan band and remain alive that way, the outcome would be deportation to a death camp. All of the stories lead to Auschwitz or a similar place, if the protagonist—Guido, Aurelio, Orietta, Graziella—falls into the wrong hands. The first major roundup and deportation to Auschwitz happened in Rome.

In the archive, one can read about a little boy on Via Arenula in Rome who heard strange noises outside his bedroom window the early morning of October 16, 1943. He asked his mother what had happened. She told him that she did not know. Twenty years later, he wrote a letter about that morning and sent it to CDEC. His letter lives in the archive, inside a folder in a box on a shelf.

The boxes are full of letters and official documents, even police reports of what happened that day, but that letter helped me to ask my question: Who would have known what was happening in Italy one month and eight days after the armistice and the German occupation, on that October day, when the deportation from Rome to Auschwitz began?

The little boy heard noises, and then he asked his mother what he had heard. How he learned what had happened that day, it does not say. But he wanted to register his own experience of hearing. Living in his neighborhood was different that morning from other mornings, and he carried the memory for twenty years and then put it in a letter and sent it to Milan. Rather than giving details, his letter offers a different perspective, his room another vantage point. Now we know what happened that day and we can open the curtain and see: We can read letters, police documents, and books, including Liliana's, about the cities and their deportations. We can begin to see what the little boy heard.

Meeting with Liliana again in her den, I started by asking her about details of the event itself, in Rome on October 16, 1943, the first major roundup in Italy. "The action was the same in Paris in July 1943. It was a *rafle*, in French one says *rafle*, that means roundup," she told me. The SS officer who had organized it in Paris was the same one who came to organize it in Rome. His name was Captain [Theodor] Dannecker.

"Dannecker had a small group of men, eight or ten, with him in a hotel. It was the same system: He stayed in a hotel for ten days, had a map of Rome, had divided Rome into zones (*quartieri*), and organized it all: how many men, which streets must be closed, which trucks, at what hour—all in this way. For the roundup itself, it was the German Police, called the Polizia dell' Ordine: not the SS, truly normal, normal German police. There were about 165 of them, some who were already in Rome; others were sent from various posts."

They pulled Jewish residents of all ages from their homes and herded them into trucks waiting in the streets. The trucks were driven to a nearby Italian military academy. Some of the arrested were released. Two days later, on October 18, a sealed train, with 1,020 people on board, departed for Auschwitz, arriving there five days later.

Years later, after much research, Liliana continued to add to her work, her research and publications on this day. She sites documents that show the original planned destination for Roman Jews was Mauthausen, which was a concentration camp but not a death camp. She offers ideas as to why the plan changed. They were deported directly to Auschwitz. Is it possible, she posits, that the non-reaction from the Holy See made the Germans realize they would get away with deporting Roman Jews to Auschwitz? That is one possibility.

Jews had lived in Rome since before the time of Julius Caesar. Then, in 1555, a neighborhood was established as the ghetto where Roman Jews were required to live on and off for the next three hundred years. By 1943, Jews were living throughout the city—Rome had had a Jewish mayor and Italy a Jewish prime minister, but this neighborhood and the one just across the river, Trastevere, and the city were still home to the eight thousand Roman Jews. In 2007, walking the old ghetto's main street, Via Portico D'Ottavia, there were several restaurants popular with tourists. The street's flavor retained something real, even with the tourists and shops. It is anchored by the art nouveau dome of the synagogue built in 1904, which faces in the other direction—to the river—and the Portico d'Ottavia, which was started in 146 BCE, and completed by Augustus and dedicated to his sister in 23 BCE.

Now one sees walking tours and restaurant goers file by. But even when the street is busy, there is a stillness, and an echo of that stillness.

By late afternoon that day, October 16, 1943, the Jews who remained free in the city were hiding. Even in a city the size of Rome, neighborhoods are made up of people who see each other every day, in the bakery or on the bus. This street and others were emptier. Who knew what had happened to their neighbors?

"Nobody knew where they went," said Liliana. Many family members wrote to the Vatican to ask, 'Where did they go, because we want to send them warm clothing.'" Then, as though walking down a stairway toward some possible truth at the bottom, she elaborated.

"Let me begin at the top. Mussolini knew something but not all. But one time he met with Himmler in Italy, in 1942, and he was made to know what was happening. Then, Italy invaded Yugoslavia, and the Jews in Yugoslavia had been treated very, very badly, and the Italian diplomats told the minister of foreign affairs what they had seen. Therefore, the minister of foreign affairs knew." (The minister of foreign affairs was Mussolini's son-in-law, Galeazzo Ciano.)

The German military invaded Russia, and Italian soldiers were there with them. These soldiers told what they had seen when they returned to Italy in 1942. Liliana said the Pope sent a special envoy to the war zones to see what was happening, and they came back and reported what they saw.

(See a note below about a special convening in October, 2023, and the new information from the Vatican archives.)

In a paper published many years after we met, Liliana reported on a few others who would have known. The highest-ranking Italian authorities knew, in particular those in occupied

Rome. Germans had asked these authorities to put 15–20 Italian officers at their disposal, she wrote. They were sequestered so they could not communicate to others what was happening, but in the end, they were allowed to return to their homes.

Radio Londra, forbidden but widely listened to, reported on the concentration camps, she said. Primo Levi, the Jewish scientist and partisan who was deported to Auschwitz and after the war wrote exhaustively about his experience, had heard about the camps on Radio Londra. But that news could have been considered enemy propaganda, as in the previous war, when atrocities reported by the enemy often turned out to be false.

And finally, Liliana said, a report about these camps would have been absolutely unbelievable—*incredibile* is the Italian word. And so, she said, when they began the deportation in Rome, it was a surprise.

Once again, this is what happened in Rome: Two days after they were rounded up, on October 18, those 1,020 Roman Jews were put on a train and sent directly to Auschwitz. Most were killed on arrival; 17 survived. The fact that the others of the 8,000 were spared was not due to the actions of government officials, but neighbors, friends, and others.

"Until November, that is to say, September, October, and all of November, the Germans did it all themselves, with this squad. After, we believe, in agreement with the Fascist and German governments. After November 30, 1943, the Italian police began too. And this was very dangerous." Italian police were actively participating in the arrests.

Liliana's historical research is detective work. Using pieces of information—a letter from one government agency to another about a particular arrest; a police department's list of arrestees; a diary; an eyewitness account written in a letter from one family member to another—Liliana and her colleagues assembled the history. Appendices and notes filled with data, sometimes in German, usually in Italian, fill half the pages of a printed book, *The Jews of Mussolini's Italy* by Michele Sarfatti. Sometimes the information gets passed back and forth among scholars; book titles fill some of those index pages.

In her paper, *The Decision-Making Process of the Roundup of the Jews of Rome (October 1943): A Historiographic Revisitation Based on OSS (Office of Strategic Services) Documents*, she sites documents that live in the National Archives, in Maryland. "These are documents that were produced by the British Secret Intelligence Service (SIS) and handed over to the American Office of Strategic Services (OSS) during World War Two." The work of understanding exactly what happened continues.

The days I visited the Archivio Centrale di Stato (the Italian State Archive in Rome), in order to learn about the information the state had been collecting about Camillo and Adriano Olivetti, I got a glimpse of such work. One must already know so much in order to do the research in a place like this. The documents are there, in deep storage, and must be requested. The bounty is worth it: hours after you have requested it, a letter written about the very person you are studying appears on the shelf where you pick it up, and it shows exactly what the authorities thought of him: a socialist and therefore under suspicion, and that he is a Jew is mentioned, too. This one little piece of information says almost nothing by itself, but pieced together with other letters and documents, someone like Liliana or Michele can understand.

Sometimes, as described by Liliana in *The German Occupation and the Jews of Rome*, researchers had to wait for material from Germany to become available to learn very particular details about the deportations. In other cases, the evidence of the policy making and implementation was within Italy already, in the government records there.

On November 14, 1943, the Letter of Verona, with eighteen points about the new Repubblica Sociale Italiana, Mussolini's new Fascist domain set up by Germans in Northern Italy after they occupied the country and freed him from his prison, stated that "during this war, Jews belong to an enemy nationality."

Before the occupation, Italian Jews were not deported. Now, just three months after the beginning of the occupation, Italian Fascists are told to seek and arrest. Later that month, a police order from Minister of the Interior Guido Buffarini Guidi, elaborated: the possessions of Jews would be confiscated, and they would be arrested. Yes, deportations had already occurred, but now the Italian Fascists would participate in arrests. At this point, Liliana says, the situation for Jews became more dangerous than it had been prior to November, because once the Italian Fascist police got involved, the barriers to determining who was Jewish, to knowing habits and subtleties, and knowing the people themselves, disappeared.

Primo Levi and Fossoli

Twenty-one years after Primo Levi was arrested, he wrote a letter to CDEC, on December 5, 1965. I was surprised to see his name on a letter in a box. In it, he describes the day of his deportation:

> I was assigned to the Fossoli Camp, January 27, 1944. The camp was under the supervision of the Pubblica Sicurezza Italiana; at the moment of my arrival, it contained about 350 Italian and foreign Jews. Around February 15, about 10 soldiers of the SS arrived, Germans, one a German marshal, indeed

of the SS; they discharged the Italian functionaries and then directly organized the deportation. They told us, through an interpreter, that all of the Jews would leave for a cold place, and that, therefore, it was opportune to bring heavy clothes, covers, in addition to, naturally, objects of value, valuables and currency. The deportation took place when the number of Jews reached 650; the very ill were also deported, among them a ninety-year-old sickly man. Those left in Italy were the contagiously ill, and some Jews of English nationality. They did not distribute provisions for the trip; however, they authorized buying them in the camp. We were transported from the camp to the railway station on February 22, 1944. The autobus was driven by Italian personnel, but escorted by the German military people cited above, who comported themselves with great brutality; punching and kicking us to hurry our coming and going and our descent from the vehicle and entrance into the railcar. In the railcar (a closed car for merchandise), there was no way to get water or take care of personal hygiene. The floor was covered with a thin layer of straw.

Back to Liliana

Of those deported from Italy, approximately 2,844 passed through this camp. It had been created by the Italian Ministry of War in 1942, for use as an internment camp for Allied prisoners of war in North Africa. After September 8, 1943, Germans controlled it. A section of the camp was set up for Jewish prisoners. When I met Liliana, she was on a committee researching and telling the story of Fossoli, and she eventually published a book about it, *The Betrayal of Dawn.*

Reading the story and listening to Liliana always gave me a sense of events marching toward the inevitable history that we know. But there were detours; she called them exceptions. "Therefore, it was a collaborationist role, with exceptions, naturally." One exception had to do with pretending to not know where someone was, or when ordered to search, working to not find someone.

By now Italians, Jews and non-Jews, were refugees throughout their own country, moving from bombed cities to the countryside, or Jews from smaller towns moved into cities or other towns. The small towns were filled with strangers. In a small town, the police could know everyone, where they were living and staying. But there were times, Liliana said, when they were sent to look for Jews, and they would look but not find.

I asked her about these police who looked but did not find. "Perhaps there were those who were not enthusiastic about their task," I said.

"No, they were not enthusiastic, even those who carried out the orders, they were not enthusiastic. No one was enthusiastic about this work."

I asked it differently. "Those who did find and then arrest Jews, they were not enthusiastic?"

"No," she said. "At times, they were very kind. There was a case in which two police arrested a young woman and took her to Fossoli, went with her in the train, one on one side and one on the other side, the girl in the middle. And the police were very kind. One of them took her into a station for a cup of coffee: this for the deported one. It was a contradiction. You understand?"

"Did the Italian police arresting Jews beat them, as seemed to be a protocol that I had read about in deportations?" I asked.

"No, absolutely not, she said, "and neither did the French nor the Belgians, or others in occidental Europe. Absolutely not," she repeated. "But of course, this was also a little disorienting. You don't understand when you are being deported and you are being bought a cup of coffee. It is impossible to understand. But enthusiasm, no."

I do not know what I had expected, but I was surprised when I heard Liliana speak about it. That they did not do it with enthusiasm and hatred might have made me feel hope. A part of me was always looking for hope. But I did not find it here, because there was something tragic about a person participating without conviction.

One historian, upon reading this selection, above, asked me to consider the complexity of my question about attitude, or enthusiasm. What was I looking for with this question? Did lack of enthusiasm imply lack of anti-Semitism or lack of responsibility, she asked.

I would say, no. How we feel—enthusiastic or not enthusiastic—when we act is not what matters. If we act alongside perpetrators of violence, we are guilty.

And this train of thought brings me back to Signora Ajo, to her admonition to students to become involved in their society now, at the smallest level, and to speak if they see something is wrong. In other words, practice being a citizen. By the time those Italian police arrested Jewish Italians, in 1943, they had lived with Fascism and dictatorship for many years, and in some cases, for most of their lives. By remaining in their jobs during the occupation, they put themselves in the position, in October, November, and especially in December, after the Fascist meeting in which Jews were named as the enemy, of becoming perpetrators.

Many of us wonder who we might have been in those circumstances. We hope we would have been honorable. Nora Krug, author of *Belonging: A German Reckons with History and Home,* in discussing her work, says this question is not useful. She asks: Who am I now? Who am I today?

At the time of this writing, new information exists. Pope Francis opened the archives of Pius XII in 2019. As scholars gain access and conduct research, new research points to knowledge that Pope Pius likely had about the atrocities. From the *New York Times*, September 16, 2023, information about CDEC historian Michele Sarfatti's research:

> Mr. Sarfatti, whose most recent research focuses on documentation from 1942, identified by some scholars as "the bloodiest year of the Holocaust," said the Holy See received reports that year about the atrocities from innumerable sources: priests returning to the Vatican from trips, local clergy, papal nuncios, politicians from occupied countries, citizens, Jewish groups and rabbis.
>
> "Many people were writing to the Holy See describing what was happening," Mr. Sarfatti said.
>
> At the beginning of 1942, few people, including Jews, understood that Hitler wanted to exterminate the Jews. But as the year progressed, "there was a growing association between the words 'Jew' and 'death' in these reports—that in itself should have given a sense of what was going on," he said.

As of this writing, on October 10, 2023, a convening is in progress in Rome to discuss the opening of the archives and its significance for Jewish-Christian relations. *New Documents from the Pontificate of Pope Pius XII and their Meaning for Jewish-Christian Relations: A Dialogue between Historians and Theologians,* is being held October 9–11, 2023, to bring together a group of theologians and scholars, including those from CDEC, Christians and Jews, who will study together to deepen their knowledge. The meeting includes representatives from five institutions, including Yad Vashem, CDEC, the United States Holocaust Memorial Museum, and Saint Leo University.

Mothers on Bicycles

AFTER READING ABOUT THE October 16 deportation, talking with Liliana about it and others, at CDEC, I pulled down on the pulley rope to open the shutter, picked a box and brought it to the little desk, opened it, and began to read files. I ran across handwritten lists of arrestees, assembled by the State Police in Rome. The list I saw, on lined pages, had names and addresses from the Flaminio neighborhood, one of the first neighborhoods that I visited in Rome, in 2000 to see the church of Father Ribezzi. They were lists in neat, careful handwriting, orderly, apparently written with plenty of time.

After an aimless three hours of reading lists, letters, journals, and government documents, I decided to take a break and eat my lunch in Parco Sempione. I walked to the heart of the park and sat on a bench. Full of stories about 1938 and 1943, I watched the life passing in the busy park. I found myself watching parents—mothers and fathers—collecting their children from school. Perhaps they would go and have lunch together at home. Children being picked up from school by parents.

In my mind, I saw the Jewish children in 1938, excluded from public schools, crossing this park on their way to their new Jewish school on Via Eupili.

I walked to the entrance of a Napoleonic Arena that anchored one side of the park, and read a plaque affixed to the wall of the arena, marking the spot of a Nazi massacre. A wide gravel path, now used by runners, circled the arena.

On paths throughout the park, mothers on their bicycles signaled with their bells to pass a person walking or to pass another bike. A remarkable part of life in this central part of the city was the mothers on bicycles, usually a smartly dressed woman on her way to work with a small child in a jump seat. An irritated cab driver complained to me about the bicycle as the modern baby carriage here.

Watching, I saw the Jewish mothers who had just learned that their children would be excluded from public school; mothers with soldier sons hiding from the occupying Germans in attics, in friends' attics or church basements. Mothers making decisions: where to find food; when to leave one hiding place for another one; when to hide the old name and teach children the new one. So many decisions to make, while bombs fall and ruin the city. Who wouldn't hear every sound, when every bell or crunched stone could be death.

The women now fix their stares ahead as they pass each other. They are lovely, and full of worries about making a living and getting here and there on time.

Parco Sempione was an oasis, as a park can be for a stranger who feels alone and in this most public of places can sit and watch and be with people, even if at a distance.

One day, I walked to the park to escape the sadness of the stories I was reading in the archive. I had discovered a series of drawings made by a survivor of Auschwitz. The effect of the sticklike but somehow realistic drawings was visceral; I felt sick. That day, in the park, I almost prayed, but instead asked myself, Why am I doing this? Why am I reading about such sadness when there is so much beauty here? From inside, a word came to surprise me: *healing*. I had no idea what it meant, but I felt better.

I took a long walk through the center of the city, and then on the tram heading back toward CDEC, I saw a demonstration with a group of people standing around a burning camouflage painted jeep outside the Cadorna train station. I had seen another anti-Iraq war demonstration with a burning jeep when I passed a little quiet square, earlier in my stay in Milan. I had been walking and did not linger. On the tram, filled with images, I went back to my apartment.

Marco Szulc

Alone, one notices more, and follows leads that might not have been seen if with another person. Dr. Bill and Daniela invited me to another event sponsored by their Reform group, a presentation given by the leader of the Shoah Foundation's Visual History Archive research in Italy, Doris Felsen Escojido.

Doris' parents were survivors of Auschwitz, and she was dedicated to her research on both Jewish and political deportees. We met a few times, once in her apartment, and then she sent me information about a man who was leading a growing group in Italy called the Children of the Shoah, Figli della Shoah, Marco Szulc.

Marco agreed to meet me at the rest home where his mother lived. His father had died ten years earlier. Walking toward the building, I saw a few old men sitting outside on benches, and then inside, men and women sitting in a lobby community room. Marco met me inside the door and led me to a large bright room with windows along one wall and a long table, where I sat on one side, he on the other. He was on his way home from work, he told me, and after our meeting he would visit his mother.

He unpacked booklets and DVDs from his bag onto the table as he sat. The pile waited to be explained.

Athletic looking, with slightly receding light brown hair, Marco spoke quickly in fluent English, rattling off the accomplishments of Children of the Shoah based here in Milan, out of his home and his computer. They had started as three people, then seventy, and were up to two thousand members, he said, but the major part of the work was done by a few volunteers, led by his wife Silvia and himself, who wrote and edited the publications, made telephone calls, and sent emails at night and on weekends.

It was his father's story of Auschwitz that lived inside him, that spurred him to do this work. "Before my father died he told me, 'Don't hate anybody. Just remember. Do something to remember.' So, I was thinking, what can I do to make this kind of remembrance?"

Sixty years after the Shoah, he had all that he needed to make educational materials. What had been started in Rome, then Venice, and then at CDEC in Milan, sixty years before, with a suitcase full of photos, letters and documents, was by now the full archive, with historians, a library, and thousands of pieces of history in boxes. The historians, like Liliana, published books, made films, and went around the country and traveled the world to talk about the Shoah in Italy. So, the Children of the Shoah started with this groundwork, thousands of documents and photographs from which to draw their material. But he wanted more.

"Here the CDEC is doing a lot, but they are mostly an archive. We wanted to do something that people should know. To go outside, open."

The group started by getting a national day of commemoration. They sought the help of some politicians, and a law was passed, he said, marking the day, January 27, as the National Day of Memory. People from CDEC were also involved. "It was not easy, because, as you know, they say in Italy nothing happened. The Shoah was very mild. So, since 2000, we have the Memorial Day, the twenty-seventh. Throughout the country, schools and other organizations lead talks, hold events, screen films, and even take trips to Auschwitz, to remember."

When he was very young, Marco used to hear his father screaming in the night, and he remembers at six years old asking his mother about it. She talked with Marco about his father's experience in Auschwitz. His father talked about it less.

"He told me he was in Auschwitz. But he told me, 'There were things that happened there that I will never be able to tell you.'"

As we sat across from each other in his mother's rest home and he talked, it seemed to me that his mission was about his father's wish for him to do something to remember, and it was also about himself. "Are you working out something inside you?" I asked, apologizing if my question was too personal.

"I feel I am a son of the Shoah. I do feel different inside from others who didn't have this experience, because there is something, which I cannot really figure out, but I am somehow different from the others. It leaves a scar inside, which you will never erase. I will say the third generation, my children, they also feel something."

More research is happening about the transmission of this trauma from generation to generation. But while he talked about the day of memory, I was reminded of something that I had read by historian James Young:

> As ordered by the Jewish calendar, time offers itself as an insuperable master plan by which Jewish lives are lived, past history remembered and understood. For only time, when patterned after the circular movements of earth around the sun, and moon around the earth, can be trusted to repeat its forms perpetually.
>
> Grasped and then represented in the image of passing seasons, in the figures of planting and harvest, cycles of time have traditionally suggested themselves as less the constructions of human mind than the palpable manifestations of a natural order. As a result, both our apprehension of time and the meanings created in its charting seem as natural as the setting sun, the rising moon. By extension, when events are commemoratively linked to a day on the calendar, a day whose figure inevitably recurs, both memory of events and the meanings engendered in memory seem ordained by nothing less than time itself.

Marco's task then was to use the cycles of time to honor the memory of his father, by teaching others what had happened; and also, to try to use the passing time, the day "whose figure inevitably recurs," to heal. A day of memory would recur every year, as it now does it in Italy: Every year, all the cities and big towns in Italy, they do something. (In fact, all these years later, as I write, I know that the events and their planning begin in

December and go well into February, with the Memorial, and CDEC, and other organizations.)

As reliable as time might be, though, a commemorative day was not enough. The group wanted something lasting, a permanent witness. At the time that they were thinking about what it might be, the Comunita' di Sant'Egidio (Church of St. Egidio) in Milan had already found it for them. For thirteen years, that church had been holding an annual service at the Milan train station to commemorate the deportations from there in 1943–1945.

The groups connected. Children of the Shoah and the historians at CDEC, with St. Egidio, determined exactly from which place at the station the deportations had taken place. From that area, from 1943 to 1945, trains went to Auschwitz Birkenau. "So, we got this area; the president of the Italian Republic came here," Marco stated in his clipped way, clearly proud. It took some doing—the Italian Railway had plans for that space (Marco says a supermarket)—but eventually, they gave the group the space, in 2004, and they formed a special nonprofit organization to oversee and raise money for the project. Plans began for the design.

This space would not be a museum, but a memorial, exactly at the site from where the trains left.

"When you look at the railway station from the front, the right side, you have to go straight about a hundred meters, and the entrance is below the level." Marco drew a few lines. "This is the level, but we are below the level [of the platforms.] So, what they did, the Nazis, they would carry each truck with an elevator up, make a big convoy and send.

"These are the two main things that our association did for Italy. Now together with us, other people have joined, which means the Commune di Milano, the Region, the CDEC, the

President of the Italian Republic, all together." While the site is designed and built, and money raised, a period of an unknown number of years, Marco and Silvia continue their work with teachers and students. "We hope, even if we have ten students, that one out of ten will understand and will say what happened. For us, that would be a big success."

Marco is full speed ahead. I know he has worked all day as a pediatrician. I am a part of this work, though, what he does during evenings and weekends. He must tell me everything in order to realize his father's wish: "Just do something to remember." I am one of those one in ten that he hopes will be moved by his story and do something too. The heap of educational materials on the table will help me to learn.

But Marco also helps me to begin to understand my own role in the telling of his story and these stories. "The Shoah is not something you can explain by an historical point of view. What's important is the human point of view," he says. "I don't care about the dates. Every story is a big story. It is important what they lived and what they have to say."

Marco doesn't have to worry about dates, because so much of the basic research has been done. As I do not have to worry about the staccato interview that Liliana had to do in order to get the record, with her intense attention to detail, the pressurized environment of the interview, where the interviewee was constrained to stay on task: because of this intensive interviewing, and hundreds of hours of document research, the record is already there too.

Now his group will do something with it. In Italian, the word *realizzare* can mean "to make something, to achieve something." In English, "realize" means something else, to come to understand; but now the two meanings seem to come together for the full meaning of the word: to realize in this case is to make real that which exists, for understanding. Liliana and her small team realized an archive from thousands of pieces of paper, thousands of memories, and they built the foundation for Marco's work. Now Marco's group will make something; a memorial, in stone and brick and glass, will be realized.

He is impatient. The memorial, the permanence, may help him to relax. But somehow, he must catch up with time, get something done, something public.

Marco's burden is his story: how he deals with the burden of having heard these stories, the screaming, how he saw his father's scars at the seaside, and how he does something to remember. He passes his father's words on to me: "Don't hate anyone, just do something to remember."

I am an outsider telling his story. I have always felt inadequate because of this status. Why are you doing this, people would ask. You are not Jewish, a few have reminded me. Marco is giving me his time and hoping that I will be one of the one in ten, and I feel his trust, or at least his hope, as well as a passing of some responsibility from him to me. Marco did not ask why: he wants me to be interested, and he does not question it.

Marco is unusual, I suggest to him. Not all children of survivors grow up knowing so much about their parents' experiences. "Probably because I started asking questions. When I saw my father when he was at the seaside, I saw his body, I started asking and they started talking."

Marco also wants to remember the father who played in the sand and water with his children and grandchildren, and for me to know this part too. Before he died, his father was close to Marco's two young children. "If you saw my father, you couldn't tell he was in Auschwitz. He was always very happy, smiling. During the day. But then during the night everything came out. Or when we were sitting together at the table. Why do you leave some food on the plate. You know I was in the camp and whatever, the starving, and so on."

Raised in Poland, Marco's father had two sisters and one brother. From there, they were all deported to concentration camps. After the war, a refugee area had been set up on Via Unione in Milan, and his father went there. One day, he was walking along the street and saw his brother walking toward him.

"Can you imagine? Meeting him that way? So my uncle was in Buchenwald, my father was in Auschwitz. The rest of his family was killed in the camps."

Marco's father had hoped to eventually go to Israel or to Brazil, but ended up staying in Milan, where he met his future wife, another Polish refugee whose family had moved to Russia before the war and then to Milan after it was over. Marco was born in Milan. "Now that my father is not here," he said, "I would like to know even more about the family. It's very difficult to get information. I am looking."

He said his father was very religious. I asked if he had been religious before Auschwitz, and Marco told me that he had been religious and remained so, that his trust in God did not change. "He said the fault was the men's fault, not God's fault."

Stories are invisible, but they are real nonetheless. In our ordinary lives we have such stories to remember, but with war and trauma such as Marco's father lived, they tear at the psyche. The child is torn; even the listener is torn. Marco has promised to carry this story, and if he gives it to me, it goes inside me too. I can help him to do something, to honor the burden given to him by his father, if I do something with it.

"Because I think even people who are not children of the Shoah, they are still children of the Shoah, whoever was born after the war, has something from the war, in a certain way."

I cannot help but wonder if Marco's choice of work, healing children, is part of his mission to do something to remember too. Putting a bandage on a child's wound or advising a parent about the best medicine is completely the opposite of what happened to the children in the Shoah.

As I left, he pointed to the pile of books and DVDs, and told me that books would outlive everything. We were finished with our conversation, and I said that I wished I had met him sooner. "We have started now," he assured me.

Walking from the rest home I remembered a moment walking in the park, not long before meeting Marco, when I was discouraged about my work.

Now walking from the rest home, I was full of Marco's story and his gift, his trust, his story and his father's story.

Walking, I noticed the jasmine climbing up the walls. The old plant pushes out new green shoots and eventually white delicate blossoms. The roots, the woody stems, and the young shoots are the certain seasons. The gardener and some passersby will welcome the spring green, see the new growth, and recognize the storms.

Part Three: A Postlude

The Memorial, and
an Architect's Story

AFTER 2007, an immediate challenge appeared: how to tell the stories I had learned over these years. In 2008, I went to Milan to meet the architect of the planned memorial at the Central Station. We sat in his studio and looked at the plans on his computer screen. I went home and wrote an article, published it, and went back to work.

My job and other projects threatened to bury the stories I had recorded. Who can retell the things that befell us, the refrain in a Hanukkah tune, reminded me of something I had read. Psychologist Henry Greenbaum wrote that only survivors themselves can tell. A survivor I met years later, who lived near me, originally from Amsterdam, told me I had no business writing this book: only survivors themselves can write these stories, she said.

Each year or two, at first, I went to Italy to conduct another interview, or visit the memorial site, or connect with people I had come to know.

Each year, my fiancé, then husband, and I went to Jewish High Holy Day services at Congregation Knesset Israel in Pittsfield, Massachusetts.

The Kol Nidre service is a solemn ritual at the beginning of Yom Kippur. Rosh Hashanah, the celebration of the Jewish New Year, with apples dipped in honey, opened the holy days ten days earlier. Between these two high holy days, during the Days of Awe, it is said that the book of life is open. While the book is open, you look at the past year, acknowledge where you may have made mistakes, maybe you hurt someone, mend fences where necessary, and ask God to write you into the book of life for the coming year.

Kol Nidre marks the start of Yom Kippur with its twenty-five-hour fast, and it has a serious cast to it. It is Autumn, getting dark early. Inside the synagogue, the mood is set by the opening melody and the white walls of tallit: On this night, at Congregation Knesset Israel, men—some women too—drape themselves or wrap themselves in their prayer shawls, which often are white with some blue or other embroidery, and one finds a seat amongst these rows of white walls.

Here, the opening melody is first played by a violinist and then chanted or sung. The sung melody, coming from a human voice, is haunting. The imploring sound of the voice makes me think of someone who long ago lost a loved one in a vast mountainous place. She is still looking but knows she has lost. The real words of the Kol Nidre have nothing to do with my interpretation of the sound, but it does not matter. It is a melody that stirs something deep inside me.

One year, 2012, during the Kol Nidre service, the rabbi opened his sermon with a story about his grandfather, who had fought in Italy during the Second World War. The story itself was a surprise, and during his telling of it, I remembered that my project had originated in this synagogue, fourteen years earlier, when I had gone there to listen to guest Daniel Goldhagen discuss his new book about the Holocaust. Goldhagen's talk had set me on this course of many years. I had let the project languish. I had forgotten the place of this synagogue in my project; and worse, I had lost the sense of grace that I had felt after my first meetings with interviewees. How does a person forget events and feelings that had seemed so important?

One morning soon after Kol Nidre, I found a news story in *Corriere della Sera* online about the Shoah Museum that would be built in Rome. Liliana Picciotto had mentioned it. I knew the memorial in the train station in Milan was by now under construction. It seemed that a new landscape for Holocaust memory in Italy was about to become firm. It was time to go again.

The Memorial, a Tour

Hundreds of people spill out of the train in Milan's Central Train Station, quickly filling the platform. Every day, more than three hundred thousand people pass through the station. Most of them do not know that when their train coasted to the platform, the sound of it moving along the tracks spread like a rolling metal net over the new Holocaust memorial below it, bringing visitors there directly back to 1944—most of the travelers riding into the station and disembarking in 1944, walking along these same platforms, had no idea what was happening beneath them. Sound kindles memory: individual, collective, cultural. Here in Milan, creating the Shoah Memorial at the station, architect Guido Morpurgo explored the power of this found feature, sound. But it was not the only one.

"It was a find, an archeological find," he said. The "find" was the very site from which Jews and political prisoners were sent to Auschwitz and Mauthausen during the Nazi occupation. This seven thousand square meters of space in a remote part of the station had remained untouched since the last train left in January of 1945. Instead of imagining a new shape and structure, he would use what was already there to release fragments of the site's history. Guido's task was to use the concrete and steel and a space so vast that it made its own sound—a constant echo of noises not even heard—to tell the site's story.

His challenge was to use the power of the raw space, but create a design that might encourage reflection, because, he said, "To remember is not enough. We must also think."

Guido also carried a personal burden—a family story—which helped to fuel his sixteen years of work on this project.

Guido Morpurgo gives the writer a tour of the construction site.
(Judith Monachina)

The best way to understand the size of the railway station building and its place in the city is not to arrive by train but to approach it on foot. From the northern edge of the historic center, walk north and east. The station comes into view about half a mile away, at Piazza della Repubblica, and the route to the building, lined with offices, banks, and hotels, gives the traveler a sense of inevitability: It is where you are headed. Via Vittor Pisani is straight, direct, and broad, with the monumental building, not so much beautiful as grand, facing you at the end. In the middle of your sight line, it seems lit by its own particular source, perhaps because of the piazza's open space in front of it. King Vittorio Emanuele III laid the cornerstone for the building in 1906, and construction was completed in 1931, with several changes to its plans and size incorporated into the final version. Its immensity lends itself to this story.

Soon you arrive at Piazza Duca d'Aosta. Walk toward the right corner of the building, and then continue along the side, past taxi stands, and then past the buses—there are several pulled in—and keep walking; wait at the traffic light and then cross a street that passes through the station complex and continue. The building has come down to human scale, now one story, still on your left. At a certain point, you arrive at Largo Safra to see a Zen-garden-like square of striped cement. Windows of a café in a residential building look on from across the street. In the early days of the memorial construction, not a person, not a bicycle passed.

Upon entering, you face the word *indifferenza* engraved in a concrete wall.

During my first visit, a grainy black-and-white film flickered on the long concrete wall across from the entry ramp, showing men in white uniforms demonstrating various functions of the then new station. Guido appeared to meet me, wearing a dark blue coat and black beret. The film was made in 1931, by Istituto Luce, Fascism's propaganda film company, he explained. The men in white were showing off a new lift for transferring mail in trucks from the street level to the level of the tracks. The significance of this new technology soon becomes apparent.

In order to understand what had happened here, Guido met many times with a survivor, Liliana Segre. He was struck by her recollection of sound, and so to embody what he was learning, he often went to the station to listen. The site lies twenty feet below the level of the main tracks and track yard. He realized quickly that Liliana's Segre's memory of sound was trains arriving and departing above her.

At the time of the German occupation, September of 1943, Liliana, who was then thirteen years old, and her father, tried to escape Italy by going to Switzerland, but they were turned back. Back in Italy, Liliana and her father were arrested outside Milan and brought to separate prisons. They were united at Milan's San Vittore Prison.

San Vittore was laid out in the shape of a panopticon. When a wing filled, Germans loaded their prisoners into trucks and transported them across the city to the station. There, they herded their prisoners into train cars, which were, one by one, loaded on to the lift—originally designed for the mail—and raised to the level of the station's track yard. Train cars full of Jews, and others full of political prisoners, sometimes in the same convoys, were sent down the tracks. Jews were usually deported to Auschwitz-Birkenau; political prisoners and former Italian soldiers to Mauthausen and other concentration camps. Liliana Segre and her father were on a train bound for Auschwitz-Birkenau.

It was important to Guido that visitors have the experience of listening to individuals tell their stories of deportation. Liliana Segre's is one of those testimonies.

Nearby, a wooden boxcar seemed to be waiting on a short track. "A model F," he announced. The small boxcar had three small metal grates for air, two near the ceiling, one near the floor. The convoy that left here on January 30, 1944, arrived at Auschwitz seven days later. "One week inside of that boxcar." Of the 605 people on the train, 20 survived to the end of the war. Most were killed soon after arrival at Auschwitz. Liliana Segre's father was killed two months after arrival, according to Liliana Picciotto's research.

Walking through the boxcar's open doors to the other side and looking left, the opening to the lift comes into view: a vertical rectangle that looks infinitely deep. The opening is the shape of the back of a tall cargo or tractor trailer truck. It is a gaping, bright, rectangular hole, with no interpretation, no plaque, no words, only an indifferent mechanical jeer.

At one point, a rumbling sound reverberated through the site as a train moved along a track overhead. It spread out over us until it covered all other sound. Everything stopped—conversation and even thoughts—while the train pulled out of the station. It seemed like an explosion at a near distance, the plume spreading over us. At first, our conversation was muffled by the rumble. Eventually, the sound of Guido's voice was silenced by the departing train. We could only wait until it passed.

We were there, then, in 1944, and now, in the present, at the same time. Standing there, it was impossible not to realize that the sound of this train was similar to the sound the prisoners heard. Each departing train above is a feature of the memorial, one that Guido did not have to design, it just happens, and its contemporary passengers do not know it.

He led me to three rows of shallow rectangular holes made in the shape of train cars, each about the size of a large brick and representing the trains carrying prisoners out of the station, so laid out as to make three timelines. One row, or timeline, represents Jews, destined for Auschwitz-Birkenau; one row is trains carrying the political deportees, usually bound for Mauthausen; and the third line is the mixed convoys. Guido referred to the rectangles as graves for people who did not have graves.

The rectangular cut-outs might have also served to settle a dispute. The Germans deported about 650,000 Italian military personnel and 40,000 political prisoners, in addition to Jews, and there was debate about whether the memorial would honor their memory too. Some whom I had interviewed thought the political deportees should be honored here, and one feared a "memory war." Historian Doris Felsen Escojido, daughter of Auschwitz survivors and raised in Milan, the liaison in Italy to the Shoah Visual History Archive, and active in a European documentation project of Mauthausen, was among those who wished to see the political deportees recognized here too. Now, the problem seems somewhat resolved. The timelines might make permanent the record of all the deportations, though Roberto Jarach, president of the Memorial Foundation, made it clear to me that the deportations, though terrible and often deadly for their prisoners, were different from extermination. That was reserved for the Jews.

When I met with Roberto and Guido, a question that I held close, appeared from time to time: Would the money going to the memorial mean the end of funding for CDEC?

Liliana Picciotto once told me that archival work was invisible and not well understood. The work of research, hunting down information, facts, and records, archive creation and maintenance, and books, several of which she has written, one of which is foundational, *The Book of Memory*, a record of every person who was deported from Italy, might not be understood. Each research project takes years, and even if invisible, underpins all other work. That CDEC might suffer financially was simply a matter of people making decisions about where to send their money.

But the impetus for the Children of the Shoah, the protagonists behind this project, Marco Szulc told me, was to bring the stories of the Shoah to the public. Could both the memorial and CDEC thrive?

In 2012, Guido walked me through the construction site for the first time: seven thousand square meters of concrete pillars and steel girders; that day, even over the din of welders and electricians' tools, the place was raw, and vast, spreading beyond the natural gaze and disappearing around corners; mostly gray, with spare natural light coming from a few windows behind us, near the entrance. As I left, I trusted that he, as Picciotto had said, was "a thinking architect," and would be able to give visitors an important experience at this site. Ambivalence about the memorial gave way to hope that both sites might coexist, that CDEC would survive, even become better known. During one visit Roberto mentioned that they intended to have CDEC's library there. I asked if CDEC knew this plan. Apparently, they did. He said the two organizations were negotiating.

The memorial project might not have happened without both serendipity and persistence. Back in 2004, Children of the Shoah, the organization Marco Szulc talked about, was looking for a place to build a Holocaust museum. They asked Guido, who, with another architect, 90-year-old Eugenio Gentili-Tedeshi—he had been a Jewish partisan during the war—proposed a memorial instead of a museum. They considered the idea of a museum as a place for making displays about resolved situations. "We know a lot about the Shoah," he said, "but we do not really understand it. The Shoah is not resolved." The group agreed to a memorial.

You may recall from Marco Szulc's story, that while they were searching for a space, a member of a Catholic Church, Comunita di Sant'Egidio, told them about something much better than an empty industrial building. They had been holding annual memorial services at the central train station, at the very track from which people were deported. That should be the site.

The groups joined forces, and CDEC worked to determine exact facts, locations, and details of the site. It turned out that Liliana Picciotto and Marcello Pezzetti, her research partner at the time, had earlier found the site, with the help of the head of the station, while interviewing Liliana Segre in 1985, for their film *Memoria*. Eventually there would be nine partner organizations, including CDEC and Comunita' di Sant'Egidio.

But once they decided on the site, they had to move quickly. The Railway Company, who owned the site, and the Grandi Stazioni, a company that managed it, were about to completely renovate the station and deemed this particular part to be commercial; shops and cafes pay their own way. This space, Guido said, was to become a supermarket.

They went to Rome to present their memorial idea to then president of the Italian Republic, Carlo Azeglio Ciampi. He was receptive. "But the government changed, and we were back at the beginning." Morpurgo and his colleague,

Annalisa De Curtis, continued to work on the design, and on the International Holocaust Remembrance Day, January 27, 2007, the new president, Giorgio Napolitano, attended an event there. It was after that visit, Guido said, that Napolitano asked the Italian Railway CEO to "open the gates for a while," to keep the discussion with the memorial group open, and not rush to develop the site. This intervention gave them time to begin fundraising.

Now a wall of names continuously scrolls, certain names light up and become highlighted and larger than the others as they float toward the visitor, and then recede, returning to their place on the list. Of the six people with the name Morpurgo listed there, just one is a known relative. Guido's family moved from Austria to Italy in the eighteenth century, to Ancona in the Marche region. His grandfather, an attorney, worked in Milan and so eventually moved his family to the city. The wall of names invites searching for a familiar name. Names in red belonged to those who survived. Of the 8,500 Jews deported from Italy and its Dodocanese islands, 837 survived.

Soon after the wall of names, a round construct appears. "Here, we tried to build a hinge between the Nazi logic and the memory laboratory. In between, we put an element," Guido said. The element began with a snail-like ramp, encircled by a wall rising to separate the visitor from the deportation site. Once inside the safety of the circle, and suspended, so as to be removed from both the sound and the vibration of the station—acoustically separated and on a special foundation of shock absorbers—is a round meditation room with an encircling concrete bench that seats thirty. Its walls reach to a single light in the ceiling, which faces east, so as to represent the important direction for Judaism, Islam, and Christianity, and to the architects, represents the sun.

Inside the reflection/meditation room, completely separated from the station, he announced, "Silence, I would like to say, solid silence."

Leaving the reflection space, a visitor might go down a level to the finished two-hundred-seat auditorium, where lectures and readings take place. Just beyond the auditorium, a library was being built on three levels and encased in glass walls, to be filled with books, many written by survivors. This glass-walled space, the most expensive part of the project, received its final funding push from the region of Lombardy. Then COVID-19 hit, delays continued. Funding was one reason for delays. The architect designed the immense memorial so it could be completed piece by piece, and this way was able to accommodate the funding waves.

Near the exit, huge metal gates hang open in front of windows to the street. "We want to open this place to the city, the city that does not know what happened here."

Guido Morpurgo early in the construction of the memorial, walks in front of the cement wall with the word INDIFFERENZA carved into it. (Judith Monachina)

Guido's story

During the Racial Laws, Guido's father was forbidden from attending public schools. Jewish professionals, like Guido's grandfather, a lawyer, were severely limited in the practice of their professions, so severely limited that many were forced to close their doors. Within days of Italy joining the war on the side of Germany, the Allies, the British at that point, began to bomb Milan. Eventually, half of Milan was destroyed.

The turning point year, 1943, brought the downfall of Mussolini, his imprisonment, Allied landings, the armistice, and finally the German occupation. With the armistice and occupation, "the real slaughter" began, as Maria Perla Ajo told us.

Immediately after September 8, Guido's grandfather moved his family to Montelago, not far from the Adriatic coast. Many Jewish families moved to places where they thought their Jewishness would be unknown.

One month later, in October of 1943, in Rome, the occupying Germans deported more than one thousand Jews. On December 5, they sent their first convoy from Milan's Central Station: Three hundred Jews were sent directly to Auschwitz-Birkenau.

When Guido began the memorial design in 2004, in his 40s, he had been thinking long and hard about people and their urban spaces, in particular the interaction between buildings and the people in and around them, designing projects from Shanghai to Milan. In 2002, he won a competition to design a small Jewish museum at the central synagogue, but that project was not funded.

His design for another memorial, this one to civilians at the Gothic Line, the German defensive line in Central Italy, in particular, in order to honor the memory of men, women and children who had been locked in their house and then burned by Italian Fascists, was stopped short due to lack of funding. He and his father, Giorgio, also an architect, worked together to design that memorial, because it had a particular significance to them.

His father, as a teenager living with his parents and two siblings in Montelago, became active in the Resistance. In addition to his native Italian, he spoke German, English, and French, and worked as a translator for the Allies in central Italy. Eventually, he was arrested by the Nazis, to be brought with other young men for labor in Germany. Giorgio's father, Guido's grandfather, bribed an SS physician, who signed a document saying that Giorgio had contagious tuberculosis. This was arranged through the mediation of a local priest, Pietro Sadori, who knew that that Giorgio was Jewish, but the arresting SS officers did not know, and so they released him. "So, for me," he said, "the narration of the memory is a duty."

Guido, like the historians and teachers who work on this subject, wants to be sure the story of the Shoah is known to future generations. In Italy, many historians think the country came late to recognize the role of Italian Fascists in the Holocaust.

This memorial project has taken longer than he had expected. "Too long," he laughed. But as he opens the door of this story to the city, he may be able to close another one. He may have missed the chance to tell the story of the partisans— civilians—who were burned alive in their home, but he has told this story, in concrete and steel.

Another train left, shaking any sense of detachment from the site, all other thoughts cancelled by the rumbling. "The noise seems to cancel the time within the space," Guido said. "It is a time machine."

And so, the journey one takes through Guido's story and the station is one of time, being there, in 1944, and today.

But the story of the memorial is not over, Guido said, during our last visit, as we approached the exit.

A final decision was made to move CDEC offices into a space adjacent to the memorial itself and the library and archive into the glassed walled space that had been designed with the books in mind. At one of the inaugural events, Guido said books all together, "are bricks in the building of memory." CDEC's move will, Liliana Picciotto hopes, among other things, secure the continued digitization process of the archives. Now, instead of the four tables together, the archive with the school student type desk and chair, and crowded stacks, the library and archive are as beautiful as a design magazine photo.

On June 15, 2022, the CDEC Library and Archive space was inaugurated. Jamie Keller, the teacher with whom I had worked on the Lenox Gubbio project, accompanied me to the event. We arrived early, and with timed tickets, participated in a tour. Liliana gave a talk at the Wall of Names.

Various guides brought us through the parts of the memorial. Inside the library and archive space, we sat and listened to Laura Brazzo and others tell us about what they do. We were pleased to see the space, to be a part of the inauguration. We went for that purpose, to play our small part by simply being there, being part of the people who care.

The main entrance to the station, with its hundreds of people, is worlds away. During the renovation, the monumental building was carved into a warren of shops and glass-enclosed escalators and ramps. If the memorial group had not gotten it first, the owners might have built a lovely market here too, far from the main entrance, at the site of the old mail depot. If this

*Liliana Picciotto speaks at inaugural events, in front of the
Wall of Names. (Judith Monachina)*

site had been glassed and walled and polished and filled with
beautiful merchandise, the sound of the departing trains would
have seemed mundane. Instead, travelers who visit the memorial
will be part of a new European citizenry, says Picciotto, one
she hopes is "inoculated against intolerance." When they later
board their trains, they will know that they are about to be a
part of someone else's experience of history, but this time, not
unknowingly, and perhaps, not indifferent.

Bibliography

Angel, Marc D. *The Jews of Rhodes: The History of a Sephardic Community*. New York: Sepher Hermon Press Inc. and The Union of Separdic Congregations, 1978.

Artom, Emmanuele. *Diari, Gennaio 1940–febbraio, 1944*. Edited by Foundazione Centro di Documentazione Ebraica Contemporanea (CDEC). Milano: 1966.

Artom, Emanuele. *Diari di un partigiano ebreo. Gennaio 1940–febbraio 1944*. Edited by Guri Schwarz, Bollati Boringhieri. Torino: 2008.

Archivio Fondazione CDEC, Fondo Vicissitudini dei singoli, Serie I, b. 3, fasc. 72., Boehm folder, Il Mio Risotto Giallo, Copy consigned to CDEC Archive, 2002.

Bellucci, Simona, Dina Castellani, and Lina Panfili. "Un Ebreo Eugubino: Ettore Ajo' Diario." *Gli ebrei in Italia tra il 1938 e il 1945: Gubbio e la persecuzione razziale*. 2001.

Ben-Ghiat, Ruth. *Strongmen, Mussolini to the Present*. New York: W.W.Norton & Company, 2020.

Bosworth, R. J. B. *Mussolini's Italy: Life Under the Fascist Dictatorship, 1915–1945.* New York: Penguin Books, 2007.

Broggini, Renata. *Frontier of Hope, Jews from Italy seek refuge in Switzerland, 1943–1945.* Milano: Ulrico Hoepli, 1998 in Italian, 2003 in English.

Caizza, Bruno. *Camillo E Adriano Olivetti,* Torino: UTET, 1962. Biblioteca G.G. Feltrinelli, Rep. 1.02.269.

Caponi, Alessandro. "Museo della Shoah, ecco come cambiera' Villa Torlonia." *Corriere della Sera,* 21 ottobre, 2014.

Chiappano, Alessandra. *Lucian Nissim Momigliano: Una Vita.* Firenze, Italy: Casa Editrice Giuntina, 2010.

——. Chiappano. *I Lager Nazisti: Guida storico-didactica.* Florence, Italy: La Giuntina, 2007.

Cohn, Stephan. *C'era Una Volta: Un Racconto del mio tempo nel lager.* CDEC file 5HB. CH–DE, 7.7.45. (His drawings in Auschwitz).

Cooke, Philip. *The Legacy of the Italian Resistance.* London Borough of Camden: Palgrave Macmillan, 2011.

Debenedetti, Giacomo. *October 16, 1943: Eight Jews.* Translated by Estelle Gilson. Notre Dame, IN: University of Notre Dame Press, 2001.

Eco, Umberto. "Ur Fascism." *The New York Review of Books,* June 22, 1995.

Foa Anna. *Gli ebrei in Italia. I primi 2000 anni.* Italy: Laterza, 2022.

Foa, Anna. *Portico D'Ottavia 13: Una casa del ghetto nel lungo inverno del '43.* Roma-Bari: Lateraza & Figli, 2013.

Foa, Eleanor. *Mixed Messages: Reflections on an Italian Jewish Family and Exile.* New York, CPL Editions, 2019.

Frank, Michael. *One Hundred Saturdays: Stella Levi and the Search for a Lost World*. New York: Avid Reader Press, 2022

Gattegno, Virginia, with Matteo Corradini. *Per chi splende questo lume: La mia vita oltre Auschwitz*. Milano: Rizzoli, Mondadori Libri, S.p.A, 2022.

Gibson, Hugh, ed. *The Ciano Diaries, 1939–1943*. New York: Doubleday Company, Country Life Press, 1946.

Ginzberg, Natalia. *Lessico Famigliare*. Turin: Giulio Einaudi editore S.p.a., 1963.

Goldhagen, Daniel. *Hitler's Willing Executioners: Ordinary Germans and the Holocaust*. New York: Knopf, 1996.

Gordon, Robert S.C. *The Holocaust in Italian Culture, 1944–2010*. Stanford: Stanford University Press, 2012.

Greenspan, Henry. *On Listening to Holocaust Survivors: Recounting and Life History*. Westport, CT: Praeger Publishers, 1998.

Hemingway, Ernest. "Notes on the Next War: A Serious Topical Letter," Esquire, 1935. From *Byline: Ernest Hemingway*. William White, Ed.

Kertzer, David. *The Pope at War: The Secret History of Pius XII, Mussolini, and Hitler*. New York: Penguin Random House, 2022.

Krug, Nora. *Belonging: A German Reckons with History and Home*. New York: Scribner, 2018.

Lamet, Eric. *A Gift from the Enemy*. Syracuse, NY: Syracuse University Press, 2007.

Levi, Carlo. *Christ Stopped at Eboli: The story of a year*. New York: Farrar, Strauss and Giroux, 1947.

Levi, Primo. *The Complete Works of Primo Levi.* Translated and edited, Ann Goldstein. New York: Liveright Publishing Corporation, W.S. Norton & Company, 2015.

Levi, Primo. Primo Levi's letter. File 5HB Nova Serie Lettera. Foundazione Centro di Documentazione Ebraica Contemporanea (CDEC). Milan: Dec. 5, 1965.

Memoriale della Shoah di Milano, English language site: https://www.memorialeshoah.it/?lang=en

Moorehead, Caroline. *A House in the Mountains: the Women who Liberated Italy from Fascism.* New York: Harper Collins Publishers, 2020. First published in 2019 by Chatto & Windus.

Olivetti, Camillo. *Lettere Americane.* Turino: Fondazione Adriano Olivetti, 2000.

Origo, Iris. *A Chill in the Air: An Italian War Diary, 1939–1940.* New York: New York Review Books, 2017.

Pavone, Claudio. *A Civil War: A History of the Italian Resistance.* New York: Verso Books, 2014. First published as *Una Guerra Civile.* Turin: Bollati Boringhieri, 1991.

Pezzetti, Marcello and Liliana Picciotto. *Memoria* (film). Directed by Ruggero Gabbai. Forma International, 1997.

Picciotto, Liliana. *I giusti a' Italia: I non ebrei che salvarono gli ebrei, 1943–1945.* Milano: Mondadori, Milano, 2006.

——. *Il libro della memoria. Gli ebrei deportati dall'Italia 1943–1945.* Milano: Mursia, 2002. First published 1991.

——. *L'Alba Ci Colse Come un Tradimento: Gli Ebrei Nel Campo di Fossoli, 1943–1944.* Milano: Arnoldo Mondadori Editore, 2010.

——. *L'occupazione tedesca e gli ebrei di Roma*. Rome: Carucci, 1989.

——. "Resistenza." A podcast. *Vivere da Resistente: Storie di partigiani Ebrei*. Milano: Archivio CDEC, 2022. https://resistentiebrei.cdec.it/

——. *Salvarsi [To Save Oneself]*. Milan: Giulio Enaudi, Milano, 2017.

Picciotto, Liliana. "The Decision-Making Process of the Roundup of the Jews of Rome (October, 1943). A Historiographic Revisitation Based on OSS (Office of Strategic Services) Documents." *Yad Vashem Studies*, vol. 48, 2020.

Portelli, Alessandro. *The Order Has Been Carried Out, History, Memory and Meaning of a Nazi Massacre in Rome*. London Borough of Camden: Palgrave Macmillan, 2003.

Pugliese, Stanislao G. *Carlo Rosselli: Socialist, Heretic and Antifascist in Exile*. Cambridge, MA: Harvard University Press, 1999.

Ramati, Alexander. *The Assisi Underground: The Priests who rescued the Jews*. New York: Stein and Day Inc., 1978.

Ranieri, Ruggero, ed. *Gli Alleati in Umbria, 1944–1945*. Perugia, Italy: Uguccione Ranieri di Sorbello Foundation, 2000.

Resnik, David. *War Days: Melancholy Lessons Towards Living*. Bloomington, IN: X Libris, 2002.

Resnik, David. US Library of Congress Veterans History Project oral history interview, Housatonic Heritage Oral History Center at Berkshire Community College. 2016.

Roth, Cecil. *A History of the Jews*. New York: Schocken Books, 1961.

Sarfatti, Michele & CDEC. *Dalle leggi antiebraiche alla Shoah: Sette Anni di Storia Italiana 1938–1945*. Foundazione Centro di Documentazione Ebraica Contemporanea (CDEC). Milano: 2004.

Sarfatti, Michele. *The Jews in Mussolini's Italy, From Equality to Persecution*. Translated by John Tedeschi and Anne Tedeschi. Madison, WI: University of Wisconsin Press, 2006.

Sarfatti, Michele. Ed. *1938, Le Leggi Contro Gli Ebrei*. In La Rassegna Mensile di Israel, Vol. LIV–N.1–2. Roma: with Centro di Documentazione Ebraica Contemporanea & Unione delle Comunita Israelitiche Italiane, 1988.

Segre, Dan Vittorio. *Memoirs of a Fortunate Jew: An Italian Story*. Northvale, New Jersey: Jason Aronson Inc., 1995.

Stille, Alexander. *Benevolence and Betrayal, Five Italian Families Under Fascism*. Summit Books, 1991.

Treaty and Concordat Between The Holy See and Italy, Official Documents. Washington DC, National Catholic Welfare Conference, 1929.

USC Shoah Foundation, Visual History Archive. Gattegno, Virginia. (Virginia Gattegno Cipolato). Video Recording, 1998.

Weiller, Guido. *La Bufera: Una famiglia di ebrei milanesi con i partigiani dell'Ossola*. Firenze: La Giuntina, 2002.

Wills, Garry. *Venice: Lion City, The Religion of Empire*. New York: Simon & Schuster, Washington Square Press, 2002.

Young, James E. *The Texture of Memory: Holocaust Memorials and Meaning*. New Haven: Yale University Press, 1993.

Young, James E. *When a Day Remembers: A Performative History of Yom Hashoah*. Amherst, MA: University of Massachusetts. This essay appeared first in a slightly different version as

"When a Day Remembers: A Performative History of Yom hashoah," *History and Memory*, 2, Winter 1990, and again as part of the author's full-length study, *The Texture of Memory: Holocaust Memorials and Meaning.* New Haven, CT, and London: Yale University Press, 1993.

Zuccotti, Susan. *The Italians and The Holocaust.* Lincoln, NE: University of Nebraska Press, 1996.

Index